KU-477-289

# Broken Bread

## Daily Devotions from the *Daily Light*

# Evan Hopkins

ZONDERVAN
PUBLISHING HOUSE

OF THE ZONDERVAN CORPORATION | GRAND RAPIDS, MICHIGAN 49506

Bethesda Book Centre,
551, Block 126, Lorong 1,
Toa Payoh, Singapore 12.

BROKEN BREAD

Copyright © 1973 by The Zondervan Corporation
Grand Rapids, Michigan

Library of Congress Catalog Card Number: 73-2659

*Printed in the United States of America*

# PREFACE

The daily devotions in *Broken Bread* are based on the title
Scriptures taken from the popular daily devotional, *Daily
Light on the Daily Path.*

The author has taken these scripture passages and developed around them pointed and practical commentaries
that make them applicable in real life.

These devotionals are ageless, refreshing, and present a
deeply spiritual exploration for the reader.

For nearly forty years Evan Hopkins was deeply involved
in the Keswick movement in Great Britain. His commentary reflects that perspective and biblical insight. A contemporary of F. B. Meyer and H. C. G. Moule, he was
ordained in the Church of England in 1865. Trained to
follow in his father's footsteps as a chemical and mining
engineer, he chose rather to enter the ministry and did
his further study at the King's College. All who have read
and enjoyed *Daily Light* will surely enjoy and profit from
this companion volume. This is the first American edition
of *Broken Bread,* and this classic volume is prayerfully
set forth for a new generation of Bible lovers.

THE PUBLISHERS

# JANUARY 1

*This one thing I do, forgetting those things which are behind . . .*
*I press toward the mark for the prize of the high calling of*
*God in Christ Jesus.*—Phil. 3:13, 14

This means a life marked by definiteness, simplicity of aim, and steady continuance. But is this possible without neglecting many earthly duties? Can I give myself to do one thing wholly, and yet avoid neglecting many temporal matters? Well, look at that ship on her way to some distant port. One main purpose controls all her movements: it is to reach her destination in safety. There is a good deal of activity on board. Many duties daily have to be done, calling for earnest diligence and prompt obedience. But there is one thing being done unceasingly and in this all are concerned: it is pressing toward the mark. So it is with life's great aim—in pursuing the Christian course.

# JANUARY 2

*Sing unto the* LORD *a new song.*—Isa. 42:10

None can sing the new song who have not the new life. But many who have the life have lost the song. The first thing that goes when we begin to backslide is the joy of the Lord. We cease to sing the new song. We are like Israel, who, though they had come out of Egypt, and had actually been established in the land, were now in a state of captivity. "How shall we sing the LORD's song in a strange land?" If we would be joyous Christians, attracting others by the brightness of our lives, as well as by the soundness of our views, we must learn how to abide in the land. It is not difficult to sing when we are abundantaly satisfied with the fatness of God's house, and are finding our needs met from the fullness of the grace of Christ. It is the soul that abides, that continues to rejoice.

> My song shall be of Jesus;
>   His mercy crowns my days,
> He fills my cup with blessings,
>   And tunes my heart to praise:
> My song shall be of Jesus,
>   The precious Lamb of God,
> Who gave Himself my ransom,
>   And bought me with His blood.

# JANUARY 3

*He led them forth by the right way.*—Ps. 107:7

Nothing is more important at the beginning of a journey than that we should make a right start. To be in the right way we must follow the right Guide. *"He* led them forth." When a man is in a pit, it is not safe leading he needs first, but a complete deliverance. He takes us out of the horrible pit, and sets our feet upon the rock, before He establishes our ways.

We sometimes fail to know and follow His guidance, because we allow too great a space to come between. The beginning of a new year is a good time to draw close to the Guide. The guidance that is not only safe, but happy and blessed, is the guidance of God's eye. But none who follow Him afar off know what that guidance is. "The right way" means not the right way in the abstract, but the right way for *me*. It is not written, "they went in the right way"; but, "He led them." They could never have found it, much less continued in it, without His leading. The right way is always His way. "Teach me Thy way, O Lord."

# JANUARY 4

*Ye are not as yet come to the rest and to the inheritance, which the* LORD *your God giveth you.*—Deut. 12:9

We miss the chief lesson of the passage if we take the rest and the inheritance to be mainly typical of heaven. It would be equivalent to saying to the child of God, You have not as yet entered into heaven. But this would carry with it no particular lesson. Regard these privileges as representing the blessings that belong to the believer now, and intended for his *present* realization, and at once we see that the passage opens out to us a subject of great practical importance. God has called us not only out of bondage, but into liberty; not only out of poverty, but into wealth. He has redeemed us to enter into the land of plenty by faith now. It is emphatically the land of rest. Though we have come out of bondage, there is a danger lest we should come short of entering into His rest. Many things belong to the soul redeemed and delivered, of which he has not yet taken possession, though God has already bestowed them. What he has to do is to go up, and by faith enter into them (2 Pet. 1:3; Deut. 1:21).

# JANUARY 5

*We which have believed do enter into rest.*—Heb. 4:3

"Enter *that rest,*" as it is in the Revised Standard Version. Not heaven, let us bear in mind: it is not by *faith* that we enter into heaven. But there is a rest that "remains" to us who have come out of Egypt, which we may now enter into by faith. It lies between us and glory. Not all those Israelites who came out of Egypt entered into the Promised Land. Not all who have been delivered from the authority of darkness have entered into the rest here spoken of. It is to Christians this privilege belongs; it is this that Christians are in danger of coming short of. God has provided it for them. He has already bestowed it; but because of unbelief they are kept out of it. What is this rest? Not something negative, merely deliverance "out of"—but something positive, satisfaction in God. It is God's own rest. Not a mere spiritual luxury, but the essential condition of all consistent walking, all sound judgment, and all effective service. God's rest is the center of all true action, and the spring of, all victorious power. Activity outside of his rest means fruitless effort, exhaustion, and failure. By faith, then, let us enter into *that* rest.

# JANUARY 6

*Let the beauty of the* Lord *our God be upon us: and establish thou the work of our hands.*—Ps. 90:17

May the comeliness of the Lord our God be upon us. "Thy renown went forth among the heathen for thy beauty," is the Lord's testimony concerning His people. "For it was perfect through my comeliness, which I had put upon thee, saith the Lord God" (Ezek. 16:14). To be conformed to the image of His Son is the purpose God has concerning us. Let that image be seen upon us. Let it be something that belongs not only to our standing, our position judicially before God, but to our character, our condition practically in our walk before men. The work will be true and abiding if the walk is holy and steadfast. This "beauty" is not a mere external comeliness. It is the outward expression of an inner life. Christ must dwell in the heart if His image is to be seen in the character. The psalmist prays that the works of their hands, which had been wrought in God, should by Him be made permanent.

"Arise, shine; for thy light is come, and the glory of the Lord is risen upon thee. (Isa. 60:1).

# JANUARY 7

*Think upon me, my God, for good.*—Neh. 5:19

The prayer of a willing and obedient worker. While Nehemiah went forth to active effort, he did not forget the one Source from whom all blessing comes. He goes forth, not without feelings of personal weakness, not without a sense of opposing difficulties. But let God answer his prayer, and he knew he would lack neither strength nor succor. In Nehemiah we see the union of the two essential characteristics of all effective service—activity and prayer. He was emphatically a man of prayer. He lived in it. It was not to him an exercise to be confined to stated times; it was the very atmosphere of his life. No matter in what circumstances he might be placed, or before what personages he might be standing, he was ready at all times to dart a message to the throne of heaven, and as ready to trace the Hand that answered it. What a vivid view of the man's inner life do we get from Nehemiah 2:4! What an illustration of that presence of mind which may be described as the sense and practice of the Presence of God!

# JANUARY 8

*They that know thy name will put their trust in thee: for thou,*
LORD, *hast not forsaken them that seek thee.*—Ps. 9:10

To know God's name is to know His character—to know *Him*. Had God not revealed Himself, man could never have attained to this knowledge. To know Him is to see His trustworthiness; and when we are convinced of that, it is not difficult to put our trust in Him. Ignorance of God is the secret of all our impenitence. We begin to pray when the first glimmer of the light of the knowledge of God breaks into our soul. "If thou knewest the gift of God"—what then?—"thou wouldst have asked of him" (John 4:10). "I know whom I have believed" (not "in whom," as many inaccurately quote the text). I know Him whom I have trusted. The whole Gospel is comprehended in the divine names. Let this be our prayer: Lord, show me Thyself. Let me know Thee. Unveil to the eye of my soul Thy glorious attributes. Let me forget my own faith and my own efforts to trust Thee. Let me see Thy glorious trustworthiness, and rest."

# JANUARY 9

*Thou hast given a banner to them that fear thee, that it may be displayed because of the truth.*—Ps. 60:4

The banner God has given us both as a rallying point for His hosts and as an assurance of victory. He has given us the ensign of the Gospel that it might be unfurled. Let us first be sure that we have taken our place under this standard. It is impossible confidently to display it—that is, to proclaim the message of salvation to others—if we have not realized its saving efficacy ourselves. There must be no hesitancy in our manner, no uncertainty in our words, if we would have men take heed to our call. To display the banner faithfully, to proclaim the message fully and courageously, we must ourselves have learned experimentally that the Gospel is indeed God's power unto salvation (Rom.1:16). Dr. Kay renders it, "Thou gavest them who fear Thee a banner to bear aloft because of steadfastness— "that Thy loyal servants might have a firm rallying point."

"Holding forth the word of life" (Phil. 2:16).

# JANUARY 10

*I pray God your whole spirit and soul and body be preserved blameless unto the coming of our Lord Jesus Christ.*
—1 Thess. 5:23

This verse puts before us the three parts of man's constitution. The spirit—that which alone can hold communion with God. The soul—the seat of the rational faculties. The body—the organ of our senses. He who preserves or keeps us, is God. But, before He keeps us, He takes us into His possession. In other words, before He keeps us in holiness, He brings us into holiness. To sanctify is to make holy by consecrating to a holy use, or bringing into the one center of all holiness—that is, God. We sanctify ourselves when we present ourselves to the Holy One. God sanctifies us when He takes us to Himself—appropriates, and fills us. Then comes the keeping. This is the prayer, to be kept "blameless"—not "faultless"; that shall be our state hereafter (Jude 24). Kept blameless continually right on to "the coming of our Lord Jesus Christ."

"Now unto him that is able to keep you from falling, and to present you faultless before the presence of his glory with exceeding joy" (Jude 24).

# JANUARY 11

*Praise waiteth for thee, O God, in Sion.*—Ps. 65:1

Oh, Praise is silent before Thee. "Praise waits in calm and assured faith that God's goodness is ready to shine forth, however great the present darkness. Such devout confidence is itself praise even if no word be uttered. And *there* —in Zion—this tranquil praise had its abiding home; because there the sin-troubled conscience (v. 3) was quieted, and so enabled to take its part in the anthems that daily ascended thence to Heaven" (Dr. Kay). It implies that our hearts, like a musical instrument, are already in tune— waiting for the Lord's pleasure to give forth their sounds of praise. We may be filled with a spirit of praise, though our lips for a time are silent. There is no richer blessing than the gift of a thankful heart, a joyous and praising spirit. The praise that ascends to God in vocal songs must first descend from God, in the form of a humble and grateful heart.

"I will bless the LORD at all times: his praise shall continually be in my mouth" (Ps. 34:1).

# JANUARY 12

*The only wise God our Saviour.*—Jude 25

Both wisdom and grace are revealed in redemption. We not only see boundless love in the cross of Jesus Christ, but infinite wisdom. It is there, and there only, that the full display of all God's attributes may be seen.

After we have been brought to know the riches of His grace, we often are called to show our faith in the perfection of His wisdom. Not in redemption only, but in providence, we have to trust the wisdom of God. When we see not the why or the wherefore, when all our ways are dark and clouded, to be able still to rest content with His leading and appointment, not because we see or understand but because we are sure that *He knows*—this is to trust "the only wise God our Saviour." God the Father is our Saviour through the mediation of His Son. It was the Father who sent the Son to be the Saviour of the world.

"O the depth of the riches both of the wisdom and knowledge of God!" (Rom. 11:33).

# JANUARY 13

*Thou wilt keep him in perfect peace, whose mind is stayed on thee.*—Isa. 26:3

These words bring before us the *Keeper,* the *keeping,* and the *kept.* The *Keeper* is none other than Jehovah Himself. Nothing less than God Himself was needed for man's salvation. And this not merely to deliver him from condemnation, but to keep him from falling. We are kept by the power of God.

The *keeping* is described in the words "in perfect peace." This is the nature of it—it is peace in its fullest measure and in its truest sense—inward and outward peace—peace of conscience and soul—peace with God and of God. The *kept.* What is it that characterizes them? Their minds are stayed on God. Dr. Kay tells us that the word here rendered "mind" means properly the imagination—the same word as in Gen. 6:5; 8:21; Deut. 31:21; 1 Chron. 28:9; 29:18. It is in the imagination that we begin to go astray. Let that be stayed on God, and we need not be cast down because of conscious weakness. The word "stayed" occurs only in Psalms 111:8; 112:8. "Because he trusteth in thee." This implies entire *repose* of faith. It is not mere clinging, but resting (Phil. 4:6, 7).

# JANUARY 14

*My Father is greater than I.*—John 14:28

These words must be understood as referring to the position of the Son at the time when they were spoken. The superior greatness of the Father lies in His relation to the Son as Incarnate and not yet glorified.

In the same chapter we read of Philip saying unto Him, "Lord, show us the Father, and it sufficeth us. Jesus saith unto him, Have I been so long time with you, and yet hast thou not known me, Philip? he that hath seen me hath seen the Father; and how sayest thou then, Shew us the Father?" (John 14:8-11).

This saying of the Lord Jesus, it has been well said, "assumes in Him who uttered it the most vivid consciousness of His participation in the Divine Nature. . . . So far as it was fit that the Son should be Incarnate and suffer, and not the Father, it is possible for us to understand that the Father is greater than the Son as Son, in Person, but not in Essence *(Speaker's Commentary).*

# JANUARY 15

*My soul cleaveth unto the dust: quicken thou me according to thy word.*—Ps. 119:25

A consciousness and a confession of earthly-mindedness. And yet withal a desire to rise above that condition. The words describe a soul in a state of depression—cleaving unto the dust. This may arise from want of knowledge as to God's way of deliverance, or from lack of faith, or from want of will. Any of these causes will bring us into captivity to the law of sin. The tendency of that law is downward— "unto the dust." But none of God's children need be brought under that law.

But how is it that all believers do not live in the power of this superior law? Because they do not fulfill the conditions. We cannot rise triumphantly above the influences of the world, and rejoice in freedom from the law of sin, unless we are abiding "in Christ Jesus" (Rom. 8:1). There must be knowledge—"according to thy word." There must be faith—the conviction that there is "in Christ" the power to deliver. And there must be the willingness to be delivered.

# JANUARY 16

*It pleased the Father that in him should all fulness dwell.*
—Col. 1:19

All fullness! Whatever divine excellence is in the Father (Eph. 3:19; cf. John 1:16; 3:34), or in the Holy Ghost, dwells also in Him who is the first-born from the dead. Fullness of merit, fullness of peace, purity, and power, "all the fulness of the Godhead dwells in him bodily." Let nothing tempt you to exclude from that one Fountain any spiritual blessing whatever. "Blessed be the God and Father of our Lord Jesus Christ, who hath blessed us with all spiritual blessings [with every possible blessing, for time and eternity, which the Spirit has to bestow—every blessing of the Spirit] in heavenly places in Christ" (Eph. 1:3).

What an unspeakable gift for the Father to bestow! What an infinite treasury of wealth for the pardoned sinner to receive! "Ye are complete"—i.e., filled full "in him." Lord, open our eyes, that we may behold this fullness—that we may be satisfied with it, empowered by it, and continually enriched in its exhaustless treasures.

# JANUARY 17

*Thou hast in love to my soul delivered it from the pit of corruption.*—Isa. 38:17

Literally, Thou hast loved my soul back from the pit of destruction. "As if the love of God, shining on the soul, had made it ascend out of the power of death" (Dr. Kay). Was Hezekiah referring to the grave when he uttered these words? If he was, death was to him a far more terrible thing than it is to the believer now. For he speaks of his soul, and not merely of his body, in that deliverance. If Hezekiah must sing with gratitude because God had revoked the sentence of death, how much more should the Christian rejoice with joy unspeakable when he remembers that the Lord has brought him out of a horrible pit, out of the miry clay, and has set his feet upon a rock (Ps. 40:2). Let the fact of this great deliverance be the ground of still further mercies. What He has done for my soul, let Him now do for my feet. Let the same divine power which delivered me from death be perpetually in exercise to keep me from stumbling in my walk. Thine is the power; to Thee shall be the glory.

# JANUARY 18

*Him that was to come.*—Rom. 5:14

From an Old Testament standpoint this was a description of the Messiah. But to the Apostle Paul and to us, Christ is He who has come. In a very true sense Christ belongs to every age. He is "the same yesterday, and today, and for ever" (Heb. 13:8). And in the Apocalypse He is described as He "which is, and which was, and which is to come" (Rev. 1:4). Adam was "a figure of Him that was to come." We rejoice in the fact that "the Son of man is come to seek and to save that which was lost" (Luke 19:10). He Himself declares, "I am come that they might have life, and that they might have it more abundantly" (John 10:10). Salvation has come down to the very door of the sinner's heart. Not only life, but also fullness of life, is within every believer's reach. But, while I grasp the fact that He *has* come, let me never lose sight of the glorious hope that the same Lord *will* come. I stand between His first and second Advents. We may even now be at the very eve of His appearing!

# JANUARY 19

*Serving the Lord with all humility of mind.*—Acts 20:19

Serving the Lord as the apostle understood it was a very different thing from servitude. God's service was to him perfect freedom. Note the essential conditions to the service of God:

*Freedom.* "That we being delivered out of the hand of our enemies, might serve him without fear" (Luke 1:74). "But now being made free from sin [from sin as a master] and become servants to God" (Rom. 6:22).

*Sonship.* All God's servants are children in His family. We serve not for salvation, but from it. "As obedient children (literally, 'children of obedience') so be ye holy" (1 Pet. 1:14, 15). "As many as received him, to them gave he power to become the sons of God" (John 1:12).

*Humility.* "Be clothed with humility" to serve one another (1 Pet. 5:5). There is no greater hindrance to successful service than "self." As we cannot take up our cross in following Christ until we deny ourselves—that is, ignore self—so we are not fit to serve until self has been displaced. Christ must take the center, the throne of the heart. In no other way can self be gotten rid of.

# JANUARY 20

*His Name shall be called Wonderful.*—Isa. 9:6

This word "Wonderful" may be rendered "miracle" or "wonder." The same word occurs in Isa. 25:1; Exod. 15:11; Pss. 88:10-12; 89:5. The Incarnation was the miracle of miracles. This was the great mystery of godliness (1 Tim. 3:16).

Christ is "Wonderful" in His being, in His work, in His ways, and in His words. He can take the sinner sunken in sin and degraded by vice, and transform him into an heir of glory, a child of light and holiness. He can take the weak and helpless one, and in His own might use him to the pulling down of strongholds.

So in His dealings with us in providence, as well as in redemption, how wonderfully He makes the light to shine out of darkness, and the crooked things straight! Let us not be afraid to expect wonders in our life, when we have such a Wonderful Saviour to undertake for us. It is His delight to reveal continually, to those who trust Him, the wonders of His love and power and wisdom, as He leads them onward in their walk of faith.

# JANUARY 21

*Every branch that beareth fruit, he purgeth it.*—John 15:2

Can you think of a vine without branches? That would not be more strange than the glorified Christ without His believing people. "I am the vine," says the Lord Jesus, "ye are the branches." The branch that bears fruit is a branch that is receiving uninterruptedly the life-sap from the root. The believer that is "filled with the fruits of righteousness" is not only united to Christ, he is in unbroken fellowship with Him. The branch does not *produce* the fruit—it *bears* it. So the fruitful soul knows that it is from Christ alone that his fruit is found (Hos. 14:8). What the branch bears is, after all, the fruit of the tree. The branch cannot bear fruit *from* itself. Observe, it is the fruitful branch that the Lord purges or cleanses. He removes everything from the branch which tends to divert the vital power from the production of fruit. This cleansing is with this definite end—increased fruitfulness. Let us not shrink from the pruning-knife or the process of cleansing, for we are in the hands of the infinitely tender and all-wise Husbandman: His glory and our deepest joy are one and the same thing.

# JANUARY 22

*This God is our God for ever and ever: he will be our guide even unto death.*—Ps. 48:14

It is strengthening to our faith to declare to ourselves and to others what God declares to us. He has said, "I am thy God" (Isa. 41:10). Let our souls respond, "This God is our God for ever and ever." It is an important step forward in the faith-life to rise from the prayer "Be thou" to the assurance "Thou art." It is thus that we step out and advance in the spiritual life." Many for years have been *seeking,* when they should have been *resting,* as to their soul's attitude toward God. When God declares to us a *fact* it is for us to accept it and rest on it. When He gives us a *promise,* it is for us to plead it, and expect its fulfillment.

The apprehension of the fact that God is our God, our covenant God—our everlasting portion—removes all difficulty in the way of trusting Him as our Guide. "He Himself will lead us," as Dr. Kay renders it, "over death—across the gulf of death." Death is not our destination. We walk "through the valley," not merely into it, as if it were a place where there is "no thoroughfare" (Pss. 78:52, 53; 23:4).

# JANUARY 23

*Hope maketh not ashamed.*—Rom. 5:5

This is not true of all our hopes. There are many that end in bitter disappointment. They do not fulfill our expectations. But this hope does not put us to shame. Christ is the object of hope, as He is the object of faith. If we have passed from death to life we have "fled for refuge to lay hold upon the hope set before us: which hope we have as an anchor of the soul, both sure and steadfast, and which entereth into that within the veil; whither the forerunner is for us entered, even Jesus, made an high priest for ever after the order of Melchisedec" (Heb. 6:18-20).

"Two images beautifully combined: I. The *soul* is the *ship;* the *world,* the *sea;* the *bliss beyond* the world, the *distant coast;* hope resting on faith, the *anchor* which prevents the vessel being tossed to and fro; the *encouraging consolation* through the *promise* and *oath* of God, the *cable* connecting the ship and anchor.

"II. The world is the forecourt; heaven the Holy of holies; Christ, the High Priest going before us, so as to enable us, after Him, and through Him, to enter within the veil" *(Dr. Fausset).*

# JANUARY 24

*The Lord is at hand.*—Phil. 4:5

The apostle reminds them of this fact—that the Lord is nigh, standing close to them, beholding not only their outward conduct, but their inner disposition—as an incentive to their forbearance. "Let your moderation (or 'gentleness') be known unto all men." You will be tempted sometimes to assert your rights, to defend your character, to stand up for your reputation. Well, remember you have put all this into the Lord's hands. Leave it there. He is at hand to look after your interests. Both the example and the presence of the Master will help us at such a time.

"The Lord is at hand"—"in the sense of *presence,* not of *coming.* Cf. Pss. 119:151; 118:6, 'Thou art near, O Lord'; where the Greek is the same. And for the spiritual principle, see Pss. 31:19, 20; 121:5. Not that the deeply calming expectation of the Lord's approaching Return is excluded from the thought here; but Ps. 119 decides for the other as the leading truth" *(Bishop Moule on Philippians).*

"Lo, I am with you alway" (Matt. 28:20).

# JANUARY 25

*The righteousness of God which is by faith of Jesus Christ unto all and upon all them that believe.*—Rom. 3:22

What the apostle calls "the righteousness of God" is the state of reconciliation with God in which man is placed by the divine sentence which declares him just. The righteousness of God: that directs our thoughts from self to God; from our own efforts to His free grace; from the idea of attainment to the idea of gift; from the strain of working to the receptivity of faith. It is a righteousness that has a divine origin. It comes direct from God. When a man sees what God's righteousness means, he no longer goes about to establish his own righteousness. It makes a complete change in him. It turns him right around. It is "by faith of Jesus Christ: through simple trust in Him the righteousness is ours. It is "unto all": extended to all, proclaimed to all. It is "upon all them that believe." We see its universal *destination*—"unto all," and its particular *application*—"upon all them that believe." As one has aptly expressed it, "As to this righteousness, God sends it *for* thee, that thou mayest believe in it; and it will rest *on* thee the moment thou believest."

# JANUARY 26

*Let us go forth therefore unto him without the camp, bearing his reproach. For here have we no continuing city, but we seek one to come.*—Heb. 13:13, 14

Identification with Christ has two sides—before God, and before men. In the first, we find the secret of life and joy and liberty. In the second, we must expect to meet with rejection, reproach, and shame. If we glory in the fact that we are one with Him in His death, His resurrection and exaltation, let us not shrink from taking our right place with Him as "the despised and rejected of men." "Let us go forth therefore unto him without the camp." This implies something more than a mere passive contemplation; it means an active consecration. What is Christ's reproach? It does not mean being opposed and rejected merely; it means being *despised*. There is nothing men shrink from as from this. It is easier to endure open opposition than to be ignored and despised. "Here we have no continuing city, but we seek one to come." Here we are strangers and pilgrims. This is only for a while. Soon we shall see the Eternal City. There we shall share with Him the glory and the honor.

# JANUARY 27

*Ye know that he was manifested to take away our sins; and in him is no sin.*—1 John 3:5

He takes away the *guilt of sin*. He takes away the *stain* of sin. He takes away the *power* of sin. He takes away the *love* of sin. He does this for us now. By-and-by we shall see how perfectly He can take away the very *presence* of sin. It was for this purpose He was manifested. No man could put away sin. What man could not do the Son of God has accomplished. In one sense it is done already; that is, judicially before God. But what the soul wants to know is that all this is true to him experimentally. If the provision for all this has been made, it is for us to avail ourselves of it. There is efficacy in His cross for this. There is power in His life for this. He who has atoned for the offense toward God, removes the load from the conscience. He who pardons, also cleanses from all unrighteousness (1 John 1:9). What God has purposed, you need not hesitate to seek. Claim, then, at once the benefit of His mediation, and enter today by faith into that emancipation from sin which He has secured for you.

# JANUARY 28

*As thy days, so shall thy strength be.*—Deut. 33:25

There are two ways of reading these words. According to the common interpretation, they contain an assurance of strength proportioned to the need. Each day has its trials, difficulties, and demands; so for each day there is God's provision of strength. That strength will come as the day comes. Whatever kind of strength is wanted, that kind of strength shall be given. "As thy days, so shall thy strength be."

But we may see another thought in the words. Let us observe it is not written, "As thy day is," but, "As thy days." That is, as your days increase, according to the number of your days, as you grow older. Now, what is the promise given here? It is an assurance of strength; that brings out the contrast between the natural and the supernatural. According to natural experience, age brings with it weakness and infirmity. After a certain point in one's life, the older we are the feebler we become. But in the divine life, God promises that if our days are many our strength shall be great. In other words, our spiritual strength shall increase with our days.

# JANUARY 29

*Thou God seest me.*—Gen. 16:13

How different are the feelings wakened in the hearts of men by this solemn fact! To those who desire to live for God, His omniscience is a fact to be welcomed and rejoiced in; while to those who have not done with sin, it is of all things the most terrible to think of. To Hagar the revelation was full of consolation. How do we regard God's all-searching eye? Are we willing to submit ourselves to His gaze?

It is *humbling.* How much He sees in us of sin and imperfection; of shortcoming and actual transgression; of worldliness and selfishness! (Ps. 139).

It is *comforting.* He looks upon us not in anger, but in tender pity and compassion. His eye beams upon us in love. His eye is upon us for good (Ps. 4:6).

It is *stimulating.* This is an incentive to duty, to holiness, and to endurance in trial. God looks for those whose hearts are perfect toward Him—i.e., peaceable, whole, ready, in an attitude of thoroughness toward Him, that He may show Himself strong on their behalf (2 Chron. 16:9).


# JANUARY 30

*Let us run with patience the race that is set before us, looking unto Jesus the author and finisher of our faith.*—Heb. 12:1, 2

Christ is the completer in us of the faith He gives us. But it is not this truth that the passage teaches. It is not *our* faith, but *the* faith, that is the subject of the text. "Our," we observe, is in italics. The truth here declared is that Christ is the leader and perfecter of the faith-life. He traversed the whole realm of faith. He ascended the whole scale. He has gone through the whole course. He not only entered the course of faith; He reached the goal. In contrast with the whole cloud of witnesses mentioned in the eleventh chapter, Christ is the one perfect example of faith. Though all these Old Testament saints were men and women of faith, not one of them was perfect. They all broke down at some time or other in their course of faith. But Christ is the perfect example of the life of faith. Therefore, as we run with patience the race that is set before us, let us not fix our gaze upon the saints. Let us look off from all mere human examples. Let us look to Jesus.

# JANUARY 31

*If ye will not drive out the inhabitants of the land from before you ... those which ye let remain of them shall be pricks in your eyes, and thorns in your sides, and shall vex you in the land wherein ye dwell.*—Num. 33:55

Canaan was the destined inheritance, in the eye of God, of the children of Israel. It was God's gift to them even from the time of Abraham. It was to be possessed, cultivated, and enjoyed by them. Canaan is not a type of heaven, but of that inheritance of fullness of blessing which it is the privilege of God's people to possess even now. There are many hindrances to their taking possession of their lawful privileges. And there are sins and evil habits that have to be cast out, even after they have entered into these. Many of the enemies to their peace and progress come to the people of God under ensnaring colors. But here is a warning against all compromise with sin. The act of inheriting involves the act of casting out the inhabitants of the land. But when the people of God get into the land, the temptation to rest satisfied with attainment, and to let the foes remain, is often yielded to. Here, then, is the warning.

# FEBRUARY 1

*Whom having not seen, ye love.*—1 Pet. 1:8

The religion of Christ is a religion of love. It is a revelation of life, and a manifestation of light; but, above all, it is a religion of love. Love needs for its object a person. You cannot love an abstraction. That person is Christ, who is the brightness of the Father's glory.

We have never seen with our natural eyes that risen Lord. But we are sure of His existence; we believe in the reality and completeness of His work; we have trusted in His grace and favor. And more than this, we *love* Him—because He first loved us (1 John 4:19).

Those who love Him have joy in His presence. "Whom have I in heaven but thee? and there is none upon earth that I desire beside thee" (Ps. 73:25). They delight in His service. They are in sympathy with Him who has come to seek and to save that which was lost, and who says to us, "Rejoice *with* me" (Luke 15:6). They feast on His Word. It is not duty only that impels them, it is desire that draws them.

Those who know Him love Him; and to love Him is to follow on to know Him better.

# FEBRUARY 2

*Oh ... that thou wouldest keep me from evil.*—1 Chron. 4:10

Jabez was a man of prayer. It was the habit of his life. This was the secret of his courage, his goodness, and success.

Here is one petition from his prayer. It reminds one of another petition: "I pray not that thou shouldest take them out of the world, but that thou shouldest keep them from the evil" (John 17:15). After all, this is better than more territory, more power, more wealth. It is better than all temporal blessings. "Keep me from evil."

Are there not many things we need to be kept from every day? There is evil without and evil within. It is not our vigilance that keeps us, but the Lord Himself, though it is those who are watchful and prayerful whom He keeps, "Except the LORD keep the city, the watchman waketh but in vain" (Ps. 127:1). It is the soul that commits itself to God to be kept that knows the sufficiency of His keeping power. Many are trying to believe that the Lord will keep them without yielding themselves over into His hands to be kept.

Am I honest in my prayer, "Keep me from evil"?

# FEBRUARY 3

*Be strong ... and work; for I am with you, saith the LORD of hosts.*—Hag. 2:4

What an encouragement for the weak and timid laborer in the Lord's vineyard. GOD's commands are assurances of power. He knows we cannot make ourselves strong. What He requires is, that we should be willing to be made strong. "Allow yourself to be empowered. You have no *ability,* but I have given you *capacity.* Your weakness and emptiness and need are your capacity to receive. Power belongs to Me. I have the ability to accomplish." It is thus that God equips us for service. He who bids us "work" is ready, by His own might, to make us "strong."

The encouragement is based on the fact that we have His Presence. "I am not only for you, but *with* you—close at hand, to succor and sustain." No duty or difficulty can be too great if the Lord of hosts is with us, and calls us to go.

Three things are intimately associated—the call to service; the work, or sphere of service; and the power or equipment for service. They each come from God. Let us seek to let God have His right place in each of these parts of Christian service.

# FEBRUARY 4

*The* Lord *hath said unto you, Ye shall henceforth return no more that way.*—Deut. 17:16

These words refer to the time when it should come to pass that Israel would desire to have a king. That king must by no means take them back to Egypt.

Look at the text in the light of your own spiritual history. To that state of sin and selfishness from which, by God's grace, you have been brought out, "ye shall henceforth return no more."

The bridge behind you is burned. The gate through which you escaped is closed. There can be "no retreat."

This would be hard and irksome if our hearts remained as they were before. But all things have become new. New desires and pleasures. New hopes and aspirations. New motives and attractions. They very thought of a return to the old life is anguish to our souls.

It does not mean that spiritual relapse is impossible. No; the danger of slipping back—of growing cold and becoming worldly—is a real and constant danger. But along the line of God's purpose we may confidently count upon the supply of all grace, and the continual exercise of His power.

# FEBRUARY 5

*I am come that they might have life, and that they might have it more abundantly.*—John 10:10

What is life, in the sense in which our Lord uses the term? It is union with Him of whom it is written—"In him was life; and the life was the light of men" (John 1:4). Life is man's first need. There is a close correspondence between our true needs and the provisions of grace. To discover our actual necessities is to learn the nature of God's gift of grace. The one answers to the other. Christ's fullness is the complement of our emptiness.

The first great discovery the soul makes, when convicted of sin, is the need of life. We see that we are lost in Adam, and that death has passed upon all men, for that all have sinned (Rom. 5:12). "I am come," said the Lord Jesus, "that they might have life."

Then, when life is no longer a gift in prospect, but a present possession, a further and deeper need arises. There must be also that which shall maintain, and strengthen, and extend the action of life. Then it is we recognize the deep meaning in these words.

# FEBRUARY 6

*The grace of our LORD was exceeding abundant with faith and
love which is in Christ Jesus.*—1 Tim. 1:14

The order in which those three short words occur is full
of instruction—"grace," "faith," and "love." Grace comes
first. Grace is the opposite of merit, and in another sense
it is the complement of our need. It is on the ground of
grace alone we have any hope whatever. God has taken us
in our unworthiness, and dealt with us, though sinners, in
mercy and love. Christ is the expression, the measure, and
the proof of that love. The apostle, in looking back upon
his conversion, attributes all to God's sovereign grace. He
says it was "exceeding abundant" toward him. Though his
sin was great and abounded, grace did much more abound—
it superabounded. He never forgot this. It was the secret
of his deep humility. But "faith" instead of "unbelief" (v.
12), was now in his heart. It was not a vague or general
trust in God simply, but a faith whose object was "Christ
Jesus." This faith, which was the gift of God, came not
alone. It was followed by "love," having the same living
Savior for its object.

Let us ever recognize the order, and the need, of these
three great things.

# FEBRUARY 7

*When thou hast eaten and art full, then thou shalt bless the LORD
thy God for the good land which he hath given thee.*
—Deut. 8:10

Israel is here warned against a danger to which they would
be exposed when they found themselves settled in the land,
and surrounded by all the abundance of temporal prosperity. There was a threefold danger: 1. Undue elation of
heart. 2. Forgetfulness of God. 3. A spirit of self-sufficiency
and glorification.

To guard against this danger, they are exhorted to cultivate a thankful spirit (v. 10), and to remember that the
power to get wealth is not of themselves, but from God
(v. 18).

God takes pleasure in our acknowledgments of His mercies. "Whoso offereth praise glorifieth me" (Ps. 50:23). It is
not the reflex benefit only that should be thought of. No
doubt the habit of thankfulness softens and sweetens the
character. But praise is God's due. It glorifies Him. And
there is nothing higher than this—the glory of God.

## FEBRUARY 8

*Henceforth I call you not servants; for the servant knoweth not what his lord doeth: but I have called you friends.*
   —John 15:15

"Friends though they were before (Luke 12:4; John 11:11), from this time forth they become such in a higher sense; and though now ceasing to be His servants in a legal sense, yet, in the sense of free obedience, they do now become servants of His more truly than ever (verse 20; Acts 4:29; Rom. 1:1 ff); just as the Son of God was, as such, also the Servant of God" *(Lange).*

"The servant knoweth not what his lord doeth"—with the knowledge of intuitive certainty *(Bishop Westcott).* What his lord *is doing.* "At the very moment of action there is no sympathy between the lord and the slave, by which the mind of one is known to the other." But in that relation into which Christ had called them there should be a perfect understanding between them and Himself.

Christ is our example here. We are servants, though not under the law. We are servants, who have been brought into the inner circle of intimate friendship. There is a blessed freedom in service like this.

## FEBRUARY 9

*Now he is comforted.*—Luke 16:25

"As it is a great law of God's kingdom that 'the nature of our present desires shall rule that of our future bliss,' so by that law, he whose 'good things,' craved and enjoyed, were all bounded by time, could look for none after his connection with time had come to an end. But by the same law, he whose 'evil things,' all crowded into the present life, drove him to seek, and find, consolation in a life beyond the grave, is by death released from all evil, and ushered into unmixed and uninterrupted good" *(Dr. David Brown).*

The heart that shall find comfort in heaven is the heart to whom Christ is precious on earth. To the unrenewed heart, heaven would be no place of bliss, but of misery. "In thy presence," said the psalmist, "is fulness of joy" (Ps. 16:11). That is the joy of heaven. But this is also the secret of the believer's happiness on earth. It is, after all, the same comfort. It has the same source. "Blessed be God, even the Father of our Lord Jesus Christ, the Father of mercies, and the God of all comfort" (2 Cor. 1:3, 4).

# FEBRUARY 10

*The light of the body is the eye: therefore when thine eye is single, thy whole body also is full of light.*—Luke 11:34

The thought we have here is the simplicity of the mind's eye. It is called a "single eye." It means clearness of vision, without film. It means singleness of vision—the eye that does not see double, but one object at a time. It means concentration of vision, centered upon a focus. That is, distinctness, oneness, fixedness. Then the whole man is full of light. The conscience is clear, the heart is at rest, and faith acts freely. The effort to serve both God and mammon not only disturbs the heart; it produces a self-deception— a darkness comes over the soul. "It means something far worse than blindness when this 'light' becomes an actual fountain of darkness, for the man so cursed, though he walk, at noonday, carries his own darkness . . . with him."

There is nothing more necessary in our walk with God than that we should know only one supreme object of love —even God. Let us seek to have this singleness of aim and simplicity of purpose, and we shall know what it is to walk in the "light of life."

# FEBRUARY 11

*They that feared the* LORD *spake often one to another: and the* LORD *hearkened, and heard it, and a book of remembrance was written before him for them that feared the* LORD, *and that thought upon his name.*—Mal. 3:16

The time referred to was a period of great spiritual darkness. Men's words were "stout" against the Lord, it is said in verse 13. The great mass of mankind were utterly regardless of their own welfare or of God's glory. But still there were those who did cleave to the Lord.

Their *Character* is described. "They that feared the Lord." It was a fear in which three elements were combined— love, reverence, and trust. "They thought upon His Name."

Their *Conduct* is noted. "They spake often to one another."

Their *Blessedness* is declared. God delighted in them, and recorded their conduct. God gives them a special promise: "And they shall be Mine," etc.

This teaches us that it is not only energetic efforts to make the Gospel known that God notices, and records with approval. He delights in those who meditate on His Word.

# FEBRUARY 12

*They shall be mine, saith the* Lord *of hosts, in that day when I make up my jewels.*—Mal. 3:17

It is not humility to say, "I am too unworthy to be precious unto the Lord; I cannot believe I can be one of His jewels." For this is God's own testimony concerning those who love to dwell upon His name. He regards them as His own "possession" (ASV). At "that day" the Lord will gather together all the members of His completed Church. Already we are His; but then it shall be seen and known that we belong to Him. "That day" was always before the mind of the Apostle Paul. All that he endured, all that he strove to accomplish, had reference to "that day."

The remembrance of our preciousness to the Lord will not foster pride. It will produce the opposite effect. It will humble us, while it fills us with surprise that creatures so sinful and unprofitable can ever be regarded by the Lord as His "jewels." It will make us watchful and prayerful that we should walk worthy of so high a distinction.


# FEBRUARY 13

*Upon the likeness of the throne was the likeness as the appearance of a man above upon it.*—Ezek. 1:26

Ezekiel gives us here an account of a wonderful vision with which he had been favored. God is represented "as in human form," which cannot be adequately seen, while the appearance of brightness and fire and a rainbow indicates the holiness and righteousness and grace which make a glorious unity in Him and are possessed in absolute perfection—a type of the glory and grace of Him who "was made flesh, and dwelt among us."

The Godhead was revealed as in Exodus 34:10. But here God appears in the likeness of enthroned humanity; a foreshadowing not only of the Incarnation, but also of the incarnate Savior on the throne of God.

"We see Jesus"—this is what by faith we are privileged to behold; and we see Him "crowned with glory and honour" (Heb. 29:9).

We see Him there as the Head of the redeemed body, the pledge of our glorification. We are members of Him who is already on the throne of heaven, and to whom all power and authority have been given.

## FEBRUARY 14

*Suffer it to be so now: for thus it becometh us to fulfill all righteousness.*—Matt. 3:15

We can understand John the Baptist's astonishment when he saw Christ coming forward to submit to his baptism. What was the meaning of that ceremony? It was defined to be "the baptism of repentance for the remission of sins." Christ not only endured on the cross the penalty as a sinless sufferer. He identified Himself with us in our sinfulness. Our Lord could not repent. He had no sins to confess. And yet, so truly did He identify Himself with us in our fallen condition that He submitted to John's baptism. It is remarkable that Christ says, "Thus it becometh *us*." By this language He may refer both to John and to Himself, as if He had said, "Thus it becometh Me, as the Savior, to submit to this ordinance, and to *you,* as My forerunner, to administer it; otherwise your office cannot be fully discharged."

In the parable of the Good Samaritan it is said of him, in reference to the man who fell among thieves and was lying wounded and half dead, that as he journeyed he "came where he was." He did not succor him from a distance; he came down to the place where he lay.

## FEBRUARY 15

*Who can say, I have made my heart clean?*—Prov. 20:9

The question, thus put, naturally conveys a decided negative by implication: "No one can say it." "It is not a permanent purity, a 'having kept one's self pure,' that is the subject of the emphatic denial in this proverb, but a having attained to moral perfection" *(Lange).* It is this that is disclaimed. Still, there is such a thing as a heart divinely cleansed; a heart in which the thoughts, desires, and purposes of the man are separated from sin. This is not anything that the soul can accomplish for itself. He who alone can pardon sin can alone "cleanse us from all unrighteousness." Never can we say truly, in this state of existence, "We have no sin." Those who say it, and believe they speak the truth, are self-deceived (1 John 1:8). But because some may go wrong in one extreme, let us not go astray by falling into the other extreme. To be "pure in heart" is a Gospel privilege. Let us seek it, and not only ask, but receive; not only pray for it, but claim this wondrous gift.

## FEBRUARY 16

*Thy name is as ointment poured forth.*—Song of Sol. 1:3

The name of a person is in Scripture often put for the person himself. This is none other than He who is Emmanuel, and Jesus. He is chief among ten thousand. To the believer He is "as ointment poured forth." He has many names, and these are all significant and suggestive of His character and work. He is "God with us"—not against us, not far from us, but *with* us, to reconcile and to save.

To those who have found Him, the very name of Jesus is full of reviving grace. It fills the heart with joy and comfort. It is like perfume abundantly diffused. The alabaster box of ointment sealed and unbroken afforded no sweetness, but when it was poured forth it filled the house with its odor. Here is the secret of a heavenly frame, of a Christ-like spirit, of a holy life. This ointment must be poured forth *in the soul*. Every power and faculty of the soul must be pervaded by its fragrance.

Let us ask ourselves the question, Is Christ Jesus thus precious to our souls? Does His name fill us with delight?


## FEBRUARY 17

*The whole bullock shall he carry forth without the camp unto a clean place, where the ashes are poured out, and burn him on the wood with fire.*—Lev. 4:12

This was the sin offering. One of the main features of that offering, in contradistinction from the burnt offering and the peace offering, is here given us. Its flesh was not burnt upon the altar, as in the burnt offering; neither was it eaten by the priest or the worshiper, as in the peace offering. It was wholly burnt without the camp (see Lev. 6:30). This statement refers only to the sin offerings of which the blood only was brought into the holy place. There were sin offerings of which Aaron and his *sons* partook (see Lev. 6:26, 29; Num. 18:9, 10). "For the bodies of those beasts, whose blood is brought into the sanctuary by the high priest for sin, are burned without the camp. Wherefore Jesus also, that he might sanctify the people with his own blood, suffered without the gate" (Heb. 13:11, 12).

"Without the camp." That expresses the place which the Lord Jesus took for us, as bearing sin. It also expresses the place into which He was cast by the world.

## FEBRUARY 18

*Thou art my hope in the day of evil.*—Jer. 17:17

A day of evil need not be a day of departure from the Lord. In the path of the believer, evil may meet him in the form of fierce temptation, of sore affliction. There may be times when his faith is severely tested, and when the enemy makes a special assault upon his soul. Then it is that he feels his need of a refuge. He finds it in God—"Thou art my *refuge* in the day of evil (rsv).

Many have rejoiced in the Lord at the beginning, and then have lost all their peace the moment that the testing has come, because they did not at once hide in their Refuge.

David said, "Thou art my hiding place; thou shalt preserve me from trouble; thou shalt compass me about with songs of deliverance" (Ps. 32:7). It was there he made his refuge until his calamities were past.

It is not the outward trial, after all, that we need be afraid of. The real evil is the evil of sinning against the Lord and losing His smile. To be kept from that evil is to be kept in peace. "Thou shalt hide them in the secret of thy presense" (Ps. 31:20).

## FEBRUARY 19

*The* Lord *giveth wisdom; out of his mouth cometh knowledge and understanding.*—Prov. 2:6

How often in our daily walk do we find ourselves in need of wisdom! "If any of you lack wisdom, let him ask of God, that giveth to all men liberally, and upbraideth not; and it shall be given him" (James 1:5). Wisdom, then, is one of those gifts which God has promised to bestow. But more than this. We read: "But of him are ye in Christ Jesus, who of God is made unto us wisdom (1 Cor. 1:30). Here, then, we learn that Wisdom is not so much a gift we are to seek apart from Christ, but that which we may find in Him. He is our wisdom as truly as He is our righteousness and our strength. Our weakness is the sphere in which His strength finds its fullest manifestation; so it is in our ignorance that His wisdom shall be made perfect. Our need shows us our capacity. He is ready and willing to fill our emptiness with His own grace and fullness. There is a daily hearing of His voice—a continual reception of His Word. Our natural sagacity will not guide us aright, or give us a right judgment in all things. Christ is our wisdom.

## FEBRUARY 20

*He shall see of the travail of his soul, and shall be satisfied.*
—Isa. 53:11

Because Christ suffered, and was bruised, and put to grief, and made a sacrifice for sin; *because* of all this 'travail of His soul'—*therefore,* it was given Him to see the happy results of His suffering—the formation of that Church which will live with Him ever in heaven (Rev. 7:4-17), and therewith to be satisfied."

One short expression sums up here all the humiliation, all the agonies, our blessed Lord endured—not in their physical aspect only, but also, and chiefly, in their inner and spiritual sphere—"the travail of his soul." And yet it is not to these sufferings that the Redeemer looks. This shows us the greatness of His love. He looks, through all the pain and desertion, to the results that should follow. He knew that infinite blessings would be secured thereby to His people. "Who for the joy that was set before him endured the cross, despising the shame" (Heb. 12:2). That joy was our salvation.

Our salvation and spiritual welfare are a matter of deeper joy to our Redeemer than they can be even to ourselves. May His love melt our hearts and knit us closer to Him!

## FEBRUARY 21

*I am the* LORD *which sanctify you.*—Lev. 20:8

This is the divine side of sanctification. The human side is also given us in the verse preceding: "Sanctify yourselves." What is it to sanctify anything? It is to set it apart to Him who alone is the Holy One. There is only one center of absolute holiness. To be sanctified is to be set apart unto that center. We have to sanctify ourselves in our personal consecration—in separating ourselves from the evil and yielding ourselves unto God. This does not point in the first place to a transforming change within. It points primarily to a new relation, direction, and movement of the whole man. He is now for God—brought to God, and to be possessed and used by God.

And the Lord sanctifies us by receiving us—claiming us —appropriating us—filling us.

Wonderful are the effects of such a divine appropriation on the inner man—the thoughts, the desires, and the will.

## FEBRUARY 22

*What man is he that feareth the Lord? him shall he teach in the way that He shall choose.*—Ps. 25:12

The man who fears the Lord is the godly man. He may be conscious of much frailty and sin—much weakness and unworthiness. But his heart turns upward and heavenward. He seeks the Lord; he desires to be taught by Him and to glorify Him. Now, it is to such a one that the promise belongs. God will lead him in a divinely-chosen path. And more than this, He will teach him as He leads him. To know the way of salvation is a blessing we cannot value too highly; but we may have this knowledge, and yet be perpetually turning aside, because, instead of the way that God chooses, we are seeking to follow our own way. Salvation is a *translation*—immediate and complete—from the power of Satan to God. That is one aspect of it. But salvation is also a perpetual lesson of submission, going on all through life. The first is essential to the second. We may know what it is to "pass from death unto life," and yet we may thus far have made but little progress in understanding what the will of the Lord is in the discipline of daily life.

## FEBRUARY 23

*The blood of sprinkling, that speaketh better things than that of Abel.*—Heb. 12:24

The comparison here is between two sacrifices—Christ's and Abel's. The purpose of this epistle is to show the superiority of Christ's New Covenant sacrifice to the Old Covenant sacrifices. The word "better" is one of the key words here.

Abel's sacrifice was according to God's own appointment. It was altogether different from Cain's, who sought his own way of approach. And yet Abel's sacrifice was, after all, only a shadow of things to come. Christ's sacrifice was that to which all the Old Testament sacrifices—of which Abel's was the first—pointed. The types were good, but the Antitype was better. These could never take away sin; they could kindle hope, but they could not heal the conscience. They could fill the heart with *expectation* that in due time the way into the holiest should be made plain; but they could not enable the sinner to draw near "in full assurance of faith," and with a "heart sprinkled from an evil conscience."

We can never tell about all the "better things" that the blood of Jesus speaks to us.

# FEBRUARY 24

*Thus saith the* LORD GOD; *I will yet for this be inquired of.*
Ezek. 36:37

This passage shows us the connection between promise and prayer—the promise that God gives, and the prayer that it is His will we should offer. When God is about to pour out His blessings upon man, He prepares them to receive by drawing out their hearts in prayer to Him. Prayer is the forerunner of all spiritual mercies. It is God's own appointed way; it is His revealed will that we should "ask" if we would "receive." Not that He is unwilling to grant these mercies, nor that He needs to be moved by our importunity to be gracious to us. But in order that we should not think His gifts as common things, and receive His blessings as if they came to us as a matter of course, He will for all these things be inquired of. One of the chief lessons we have to learn is the privilege of prayer. It forms a most important part of our spiritual training, to acquire the habit of constant intercourse with God in prayer. It is thus that an attitude of humble dependence is brought about in the soul, and a spirit of continual thankfulness is fostered. The promise calls to prayer, and prayer brings down the blessing, and the blessing calls forth the praise.

# FEBRUARY 25

*Resist the devil, and he will flee from you.*—James 4:7

Another translation of the word "resist" is "withstand," because the thought is not that of a personal struggle, as much as of appropriation of those means of defense which God has provided for us, and which are found outside our own personal resources or efforts. To get into an impregnable fortress, and abide therein, is to have the walls between our souls and the enemy. So long as the walls hold out against his assaults, the enemy cannot touch us. Christ is our fortress. He is the armor in which we are privileged to be enclosed. To "withstand" the foe means to put on that armor and therein to abide. We do not conquer the devil, but we "withstand" him; and having done all, we "stand" and do not fall. To come out of our fortress and to struggle with Satan means certain defeat. It is in vain that we pray to have power in ourselves sufficient to conquer so mighty an antagonist. But though we are but babes in spiritual strength, we are secure—as safe as giants in grace—if only we abide within the panoply of God, Christ Jesus our Lord.

# FEBRUARY 26

*Let us search and try our ways, and turn again to the* LORD.
—Lam. 3:40

"Our ways"—that is not the same thing as our works. Our ways are our methods of action, our motives and principles of conduct. This is where the searching must take place. "Search," "try," and "turn"—here is the right order.

"Let us search and try our ways," in the light of God's presence, and by the touchstone of His Word. It is then we discover that what looked straight before is now crooked.

The true way of searching our ways is to ask God to search us. It is a mark of integrity of heart when we are willing to be searched.

"Search me, O God, and know my heart: try me, and know my thoughts: And see if there be any wicked way in me, and lead me in the way everlasting" (Ps. 139:23, 24). He begins with the source—"know my *heart,*" then "my thoughts," and lastly, "my way."

The heart can lose nothing by a thorough honest searching. We need it continually. But never let us attempt it in our own strength, or apart from God. It is at His feet and in His presence alone that it can be done.

# FEBRUARY 27

*Reckon ye also yourselves to be dead indeed unto sin, but alive unto God through Jesus Christ our Lord.*—Rom. 6:11

This is the divine command. It does not say, "Reckon sin to be dead," but, "Reckon yourself dead to it." Sin was once your lord and master. He claimed you as his slave. He demanded your service, and he is ready to pay his wages to those who serve him. "The wages of sin is death."

But Christ has set you free from this tyrant Sin. You need no longer recognize his claim. It is through death that your connection with him as your master has been broken. No master can compel obedience from his slave, if death has come and broken the connection between them. Well, it is through death that we are freed from our old master, sin. Not *our* death, but *Christ's* death, and because *we died with Him.* That is true legally. In order that it should be true practically and experimentally, "reckon ye yourselves" —not only to have died, but—"to be dead indeed unto sin." It is not a feeling of deadness to be realized. Because the same person is to be dead and alive at one and the same time—dead unto sin, and alive unto God.

## FEBRUARY 28

*God so loved the world, that he gave his only begotten Son, that whosoever believeth in him should not perish, but have everlasting life.*—John 3:16

This brings us to the fountain of human redemption—the love of God. The death of Christ was the measure and expression of that love. It was also the meritorious cause of our salvation. But it is not because Christ has died for us that God has been moved with compassion toward us. His free sovereign love is the source and spring of all the riches of grace and glory we have in Jesus Christ. How can we measure the height and depth, the length and breadth, of that little word "so"? No finite mind can grasp its immeasurable fullness. Eternity itself will not reveal its boundless limits. Then, let us remember it was not even a repentant world, or a world that longed to be brought back to God, that He "so loved," but a world in a state of enmity—guilty and lost. Let this teach me to see what the love of God means; teach me to abide in that love—never to question it, never to limit it. See the inference the apostle draws from this fact in the epistle to the Romans (8:32).

## MARCH 1

*The fruit of the Spirit is love.*—Gal. 5:22

We may have the Spirit within us, and yet there may be a sad lack of fruit in our lives. The Holy Spirit may be grieved. And when He is grieved He ceases to fill us with His fruit. It is not by strain and effort that we become fruitful. As with growth, so with fruitfulness, it is not energy that is needed so much as a healthy condition of soul. Then we must keep clearly before us the fact that it is not the fruit of the Christian but the fruit of the Holy Ghost that is here spoken of. The Christian *bears* the fruit, but the Spirit *produces* it.

The fruit of the Spirit consists of one cluster of nine different virtues. In no sense have we to manufacture them.

What, then, is the secret of divine fruitfulness? The indwelling and fellowship of the Holy Ghost. Let Christ be recognized as Lord within the soul; let Him be honored and obeyed, and the Holy Spirit will not fail to shed abroad in our hearts the love of God (Rom. 5:5). He will not fail to fill us "with all joy and peace in believing" (Rom. 15:13).

Fruitfulness is brought about not by *imitation* so much as by *manifestation*. It is the outcome of what dwells within.

## MARCH 2

*God hath caused me to be fruitful in the land of my affliction.*
   —Gen. 41:52

These were Joseph's words in reference to Ephraim. He had already spoken of his first-born Manasseh. Joseph's true home, after all, was in Canaan. Egypt was the land of his affliction; but even there God had made him fruitful and blessed him. He is thankful for the past, with all its sorrow. And so the believer today may often look back to seasons of bitter trial and affliction, and see how God has made them times of special fruitfulness. Not that affliction necessarily sanctifies the heart or causes us to glorify God. After all, it is not our circumstances that are the secret of our spiritual progress; the true cause lies in something above all our surroundings. None can sanctify our souls or cause us to be fruitful but the triune God. But He often uses our adversities to humble our hearts, subdue our pride, and make us submissive. Then it is He causes us to be fruitful in the land of our affliction. Even there we may yield fruit to God. "From me is thy fruit found" (Hos. 14:8).


## MARCH 3

*Trust in the* LORD *with all thine heart; and lean not unto thine own understanding. In all thy ways acknowledge him, and he shall direct thy paths.*—Prov. 3:5, 6

The direction is very simple, if we have a heart to receive it. Some people make experiments upon God. They want to test His trustworthiness, like a person who puts out his foot on doubtful ice. They are afraid to trust Him with all their hearts. And yet what is our faith worth if it does not venture *wholly* on the Lord? Nothing is more natural than to lean on our own understanding; that is, to rely on our own natural sagacity, our own wisdom, our gifts and talents. This is to walk by sight, by sense, instead of by faith. "In all thy ways acknowledge him." Take heed of Him. He is before you to guide and to teach. Confess Him. He calls you to bear witness to Him. Consider Him. Let Him have the first place. Give Him the preeminence in all things. Here is the secret of safe guidance, of peaceful progress, and of a useful course. The grace of simple dependence, that commits all to Him, and obeys implicitly, is what we need to seek.

# MARCH 4

*Set your affection on things above, not on things on the earth.*
—Col. 3:2

The religion of Christ is not a religion of fear, but of love; not of repulsion, but of attraction. As the magnet attracts the pieces of metal to itself, so Christ, in all the riches of His grace, draws the heart of the believer to Himself. He is our treasure. "Where your treasure is, there will your heart be also." It is not difficult to draw near to that place where our heart is. Christ draws us with the cords of love; "Whom, having not seen, we love." And is He not at the right hand of God? Does He not stand within the veil, now to appear in the presence of God for us? (Heb. 9:24). "We see Jesus . . . crowned with glory and honour" (Heb. 2:9). "Set your affection on things above." Your citizenship is in heaven, as well as your treasure (Phil. 3:20). "From whence also we look for the Saviour, the Lord Jesus Christ." Faith, hope, and love all find their object in Him who is above. Let this threefold cord draw us upward, heavenward, by the power of Him to whom we are united.

# MARCH 5

*O Lord, I am oppressed; undertake for me.*—Isa. 38:14

Dr. Kay remarks on this passage: "He (Hezekiah) is like one who is in the hand of an exacting creditor (compare Isa. 52:4; 54:14; Deut. 28:29, 33; Ps. 72:4), from whom there is but one hope of relief; if God will 'be surety for him.' " This is the literal translation, "Be surety for me." But while it is to God that he cries to be the surety, it is God who is the creditor! How can he hope to find the relief he needs in Him who is the exacting creditor? He appeals from God's justice to God's mercy—from Jehovah who punishes, to Jehovah who forgives sin.

There are many ways in which the child of God may get oppressed. It need not be through the power of any besetting sin. It may be through pressing duties, through crowding cares, through anxious fears. But it matters not what the cause may be, there is One who is ever all-sufficient to deliver. "Roll thy way on the Lord; trust also in Him, and He will do all" (Ps. 37:5).—*Dr. Kay.*

We must learn daily, continually, to commit every care, every duty, every difficulty, into His hand, and then trust Him to supply our need.

## MARCH 6

*He ... preserveth the way of his saints.*—Prov. 2:8

Both the ways and the feet of His saints God undertakes to keep (1 Sam. 2:9). How little we realize our need of His preserving grace continually! It is not the deliverance of our souls from death only that we need God to accomplish. But, even after we have realized that blessing, it is His power again we need perpetually to keep our feet from falling. We may think of the way as the path along which we have to travel. God prepares it and preserves it. It is the way of holy obedience. Along that path we shall find the "good works, which God hath before ordained that we should walk in them" (Eph. 2:10). One great business of life is to be kept constantly "prepared unto every good work" (2 Tim. 2:21). This also God undertakes to do, if we are willing to give ourselves into His hand for this purpose.

We need not be anxious as to our future, as to marking out our path and planning our ways. We have but to seek His guidance, and daily to be taught His way concerning us. He will say to us, "This is the way; walk ye in it."

## MARCH 7

*Thy Maker is thine husband; the* Lord *of hosts is his name.*
—Isa. 54:5

This relationship of God to His people is often asserted by the prophets. We have it in Hosea 2:16: "And it shall be at that day, saith the Lord, that thou shalt call me Ishi [my husband]; and shalt call me no more Baali [my Lord]." The figure Isaiah here uses is that of the *Goel,* or next of kin, and this very suggestive and beautiful illustration may be taken from the story of Ruth and Boaz.

The figure brings before us the close and intimate fellowship that subsists between Christ and His Church. It suggests, too, how precious that Church is to Him (Eph. 5:25). To be a child of God is to be included in that Church. We may appropriate individually that love which he Has for the Church collectively. But if we would take up the corresponding position of the Bride, there must a similar response of love toward Him. In order to do this His Spirit must fill us with His own love, and lead us in devotedness of heart and service. "My beloved is mine, and I am his" (Song of Sol. 2:16). "I am my beloved's, and my beloved is mine" (6:3).

# MARCH 8

*Thou hast cast all my sins behind thy back.*—Isa. 38:17

That is, where they could be no more seen. Hezekiah knew that he had sinned; he regarded his sins as having brought down upon him the sentence of death. But as God had revoked the sentence, he knew that He had pardoned his sins and put them away from His remembrance.

"When we cast our sins behind our back, and take no care to repent of them, God sets them before His face, and is ready to reckon for them, but when we set them before our face, in true repentance, as David did when his sin was ever before him, God casts them behind His back" *(Matthew Henry).*

Two other very striking figures God uses to show the completeness of His pardon. He casts them into the depths of the sea (Micah 7:19), and "as far as the east is from the west, so far hath he removed our transgressions from us" (Ps. 103:12). Then He declares, touching those forgiven sins, that He will remember them no more (Isa. 43:25).

But how may I live in the assurance of His pardon? The Apostle John tells us in 1 John 1:9.

# MARCH 9

*The living God, who giveth us richly all things to enjoy.*
—1 Tim. 6:17

The apostle, we see from the context, charges Timothy to warn those of their peril "who are rich in this world." Charge them, he says, "not to be highminded." Pride may be found without wealth; but it is hard to have wealth without pride. Instead of trusting in wealth, the apostle would say, "Let us trust in the living God, to whom all riches belong, and who is the giver of every good gift. It is He who gives us richly all things to enjoy. It is God's will, therefore, that we should accept His gifts—earthly as well as spiritual—and enjoy them as bestowed by His loving hand." "All things are yours," says the same apostle in another epistle (1 Cor. 3:21).

How often we forget that the God who has redeemed our souls and supplies our spiritual needs is the God who bestows all our temporal blessings!

He gives us all things to *enjoy.* God delights in the happiness of His children. It is when they take His gifts and forget the God who gave them that His name is dishonored.

# MARCH 10

*God will provide.*—Gen. 22:8

This was what Abraham learned in the most trying hour of his life. He learned it in the line of implicit obedience. He learned it in the trial of his faith. Could he ever forget this great truth? It is the great fact that runs through the whole history of divine redemption. Whatever man's need has been or can be, God has *seen before* and has made full provision. The fact that our wants as sinners, guilty and lost, have been amply provided for—that we can stand before God acquitted of every charge, pardoned, reconciled, justified, and accepted—encourages us to believe that all our future necessities will be met in the same bountiful way, and by the same gracious and omnipotent Savior. Let this quiet our every fear and silence each rising note of anxious foreboding. *"God will provide"* is a golden sentence to be written on the portal of each opening day. Let us show by our restful attitude and steady step that we believe the divine assurance. How truly the Apostle Paul proved the reality of it in his own life! And so he could say to those Philippian converts, "My God shall supply all your need according to his riches in glory by Christ Jesus" (Phil. 4:19).

# MARCH 11

*The* LORD *bless thee, and keep thee.*—Num. 6:24

This is a part of the Aaronic benediction. It has been observed there is nothing expressed in the apostolic benediction which was not implied in the Aaronic. In blessing Israel, Aaron was to "put the name of the Lord upon the children of Israel." It is into that name we have been baptized. It is into that name we enter when we meet together for worship. He blesses us by enclosing us in His presence and encircling us in His power. "Kept by the power of God" is the place of the believer's safety (1 Pet. 1:5).

He blesses us by causing His face to shine upon us, and by manifesting to us the riches of His grace. He blesses us by lifting up the light of His countenance upon us and filling our hearts with His peace.

All good is summed up in God's favor. David declares, "There be many that say, Who will shew us any good?" He gives us the answer, "LORD, lift thou up the light of thy countenance upon us" (Ps. 4:6).

It is "the light of the knowledge of the glory of God in the face of Jesus Christ."

# MARCH 12

*The* LORD *make his face shine upon thee, and be gracious unto thee: The* LORD *lift up his countenance upon thee, and give thee peace.*—Num. 6:25, 26

Our need of God's blessing is continual. That need arises not merely from the circumstances of trial, temptation, and difficulty in which we are placed, but also from our condition of personal weakness and sin. Our unworthiness places us in a position of entire dependence upon His sovereign grace. But God has been pleased to "lift up his countenance upon" us. These words which Aaron had to pronounce on the children of Israel were not the mere utterance of a pious wish, nor were they only a prayer. They were more. They were the divine declaration that God would give effect to all that is here expressed. God's benedictions are not human supplications. A desire expressed in prayer is one thing. A blessing bestowed by a divine declaration is another. Here then is the believer's privilege—to walk each day beneath the Lord's benediction, within His keeping power, in the light of His favor, in the riches of His grace, and in the enjoyment of His peace. Each person of the blessed Trinity is present to bless.

# MARCH 13

*There is one God, and one mediator between God and men, the man Christ Jesus.*—1 Tim. 2:5

The existence of the only God would be no glad tidings for fallen man. How a guilty sinner can enter into the presence of Him who is infinitely holy is the great fact that the Gospel proclaims. It is through "the man Christ Jesus." He is the Mediator between God and men. And so He reveals Himself as "the way" and as "the door." "No man cometh unto the Father, but by me" (John 14:6). Those who suppose that they can go directly to the Father without the Son have never seen the holiness of God on the one side, nor the sinfulness of their own hearts and lives on the other. Christ is able to be saving them to the uttermost— right on to the very end—who are in the habit of coming to God by Him (Heb. 7:25). And so it is not only at our first approach as guilty sinners, but in our daily access as pardoned and saved souls, that we need the intercessor Christ Jesus. It is as we thus come, day by day, that we alone can be receiving the blessings of His continual salvation. Let this fact teach us our true place of perpetual dependence on the grace and mercy of God our Father.

## MARCH 14

*Adorn the doctrine of God our Saviour in all things.*—Titus 2:10

These words have reference to those who belonged to the lowest grade of society. They were those who had become Christians while in the position of *slaves*. It was natural for the slave who had been brought into the spiritual privileges of the Gospel to forget his place, and put himself on a *social* level with his master. But the apostle by no means encourages such a spirit. Hence he charges each to abide in the position in which he was when converted (1 Cor. 7:20-24). He bids the slave "to have that zealous desire to gain the master's good will which anticipates the master's wish, and does even more than is required." *Not answering again* —in contradiction to the master. *Not purloining*—not appropriating what does not belong to one. It is God's purpose that even slaves should "adorn" His doctrine.

A life in which the power of the living Christ is displayed is a life in which the doctrine is adorned. If this was possible in those days; and in such circumstances of hardship and subjection to earthly masters, how much more possible is it for us to abound in the graces of the Spirit!

## MARCH 15

*Perfect through sufferings.*—Heb. 2:10

To perfect is "to consummate: to bring to consummated glory through sufferings, as the appointed avenue." Christ reached the goal through sufferings. He, who was from the first without spot and perfect, became perfected by reaching the goal.

It is as the "Captain of our salvation" that the Lord Jesus is here contemplated. Literally, that is the *Prince-Leader,* the One who leads the people—who brings them unto glory. So in Hebrews 12:2, "Looking unto Jesus, the [Prince-Leader] and [Perfecter] of [the] faith." That is, "In the career of faith He led the way, and perfectly realized the idea, and finished the course of it without fail." It is not *"our* faith." "Our" is in italics. But it is the faith *life* that is here referred to. Christ completed the whole course and has reached the goal.

Let us remember that the Lord Jesus is the Prince-Leader of the band of believing ones whom He is bringing to glory. We too in due time shall be perfected. We have to pursue our course by the same path, through the same trials, and we too shall triumph by the same means.

# MARCH 16

*What is your life? It is even a vapour, that appeareth for a little time, and then vanisheth away.*—James 4:14

These words come in connection with making plans for the future. We are prone to take for granted that our lives will be prolonged; as we say, "Today or tomorrow we will go into such a city, and continue there a year, and buy and sell, and get gain." But how foolish and presumptuous it is to assume this! For what is the nature of your life? How uncertain and evanescent it is! For "it is even a vapour"—a mere mist that floats for a little time in the air, and then disappears, without leaving a trace behind. And yet, transient as it is, how important is the mission that in our lives we have to fulfill here on earth! Two mistakes we are in danger of making. First, there is the mistake of regarding this visible scene of existence as if it were everything, living only for time, seeking only the things of the present; and, second, the mistake of regarding this life as of no importance, as comparatively worthless.

The true way is to estimate this life in its relation to eternity. "What is your life?" Is it safe? Is it holy? Is it a useful life?

# MARCH 17

*He shall put his hand upon the head of the burnt offering; and it shall be accepted for him to make atonement for him.*
—Lev. 1:4

This act was symbolical. It was the act of identification by which the offerer and the offering were regarded as one. So is it with the Christ and the believer. Faith is the hand that links the two. We are identified with Him by faith. The burnt offering typified the entire self-surrender of Christ to God. It was a sacrifice "of a sweet savour unto the LORD." So we read in Ephesians 5:2, "Walk in love, as Christ also loved us, and hath given himself for us an offering and a sacrifice to God for a sweet-smelling savour." This "burnt offering" was not only the very oldest offering, it was to be the daily sacrifice (Num. 29:6); morning and evening it was to be presented to the Lord.

Let us never forget that the ground of our acceptance is not the Spirit's work *in* us, but Christ in His sacrificial work *for* us. To take this place of identification with Christ is to confess our personal unworthiness and His supreme worth.

# MARCH 18

*Mine eyes fail with looking upward.*—Isa. 38:14

These words occur in Hezekiah's prayer. It is the language of a soul in sore distress, but whose hope is in the Lord. Life has its shadow as well as its sunshine. But even in our times of deepest trial we need never yield to unbelief. It is doubting that shuts out the light of God's countenance. Often the soul lives on its realizations of God's goodness and mercy. And then God, to teach and discipline His child, withdraws the sensible enjoyment of these blessings, that he may learn to live by faith and not by feeling. Faith rests on facts. God reveals these facts to us in His Word. Victory in trial is by faith, not by feeling. It is possible always to triumph, even in the most adverse circumstances, because the facts are always present, and faith may always grasp and rest upon them. So, even when we can no longer *realize,* we may be strong in faith. But we need to be taught by experience the difference between faith and feeling; and such is the lesson that times of special trial are intended to teach us.

# MARCH 19

*God, having raised up his Son Jesus, sent him to bless you, in turning away every one of you from his iniquities.*—Acts 3:26

The phrase "raised up" refers, as we think, not to His resurrection, but to "the whole conception of the mediatorial exaltation of Jesus Christ." God, who has "provided, prepared, and gifted" His Son, has sent Him to bless you. And this blessing consists not merely in the forgiveness of sins, but in the turning away from them. The Gospel message can bring no blessing to the sinner unless it is accompanied by a power that changes his heart and cleanses his thoughts and desires in reference to sin. This was promised to the Apostle Paul as the effect that should follow his preaching— "To open their eyes, and to turn them from darkness to light, and from the power of Satan unto God" (Acts 26: 18). The saving grace of Christ attracts the soul, and turning to God means turning from sin. As love to God increases and deepens, hatred of sin becomes more marked and decisive. This is God's purpose. He has sent His Son to bless us in turning us from all sin. He comes with power to accomplish this.

# MARCH 20

*The entrance of thy words giveth light.*—Ps. 119:130

According to the ASV it is "the opening of thy words," or "the unfolding of Thy words" *(Kay)*. In the KJV the words suggest the idea of heart illumination, like a beam of light breaking into a dark chamber. But the best authorities interpret the words as referring not so much to the entrance of the Word into the soul, as to its being unfolded and made open to our hearts, so that we perceive its meaning and behold its beauties.

Two things need to be opened if there is to be divine illumination—our understandings and the Scriptures. Both are brought before us in Luke 24:32 and 45.

"Open thou mine eyes, that I may behold wondrous things out of thy law" (Ps. 119:18) was David's prayer in this same psalm. It is thus the soul learns. The light of truth brings with it the light of joy, and the light of joy increases as we live in the light of holiness.

# MARCH 21

*Be watchful, and strengthen the things which remain, that are ready to die.*—Rev. 3:2

Like the church in Sardis, God's children often need a solemn awakening message like this. Spiritual declension sometimes creeps over the soul so stealthily that the believer has no idea how far he has slipped back until the voice of God awakens him from his slumber. It is a sad picture that is here presented. A few only of those graces that once adorned the life now remain—and these are "ready to die." A little more worldly conformity, and nothing will be left to show that the soul was ever the temple of God. How is it with you, dear reader? Does this describe your state? Listen to the voice of Him who "walks in the midst of the seven golden candlesticks," and whose "eyes are as a flame of fire." "Be watchful" against a further departure from God, and "strengthen the things which remain." Bring your sins and need and weakness to Him who alone can pardon and restore, who alone can quicken and revive.

# MARCH 22

*Lot lifted up his eyes, and beheld all the plain of Jordan, that it was well watered every where, before the* LORD *destroyed Sodom and Gomorrah, even as the garden of the* LORD. . . . *Then Lot chose him all the plain of Jordan.*—Gen. 13:10, 11

We see how Lot at once took advantage of his opportunity. Abram's proposal was noble and disinterested, but Lot does not meet him in the same generous spirit. Abram does not think of himself. He first seeks God's honor. But Lot seems anxious to provide well for himself. We must not forget, however, that Lot was a righteous man. Still, we are not told that he called upon God, as did Abram. He does not appear to have sought counsel of the Lord before he made his choice. Well, he secured a goodly portion of the land. It was well watered and productive, but settling there drew him away from God. He "pitched his tent *toward* Sodom." Sometimes God's children choose a path that brings them into temporal prosperity. But how often it is at the expense of spiritual loss! The great lesson we learn from this stage in Lot's history is the importance of seeking God's counsel and being led by His hand.

## MARCH 23

*Holy, holy, holy, Lord God Almighty.*—Rev. 4:8

A deeply-taught servant of God has said: "It is a comforting and observable fact, that the Three Persons in the Trinity are never brought together in the Bible without a result of blessing. We have instances in which each Person, standing by Himself, is in an aspect of fear. The Father we have seen clothed with the thunders of Sinai; the Son, as the 'falling stone that grinds to powder'; and 'the sin against the Holy Ghost shall never be forgiven.' But there is not an instance upon record in which the Three Persons stand together without an intention of grace. And it is a magnificent thought, that the completeness of Deity, in all His essence and all His operation, is never mentioned but for mercy" *(Rev. James Vaughan)*. The whole doctrine of the Trinity is a subject, not of understanding, but of faith. We must come to Him in such a spirit as that which fills the minds of angels when they cry, "Holy, holy, holy, Lord God Almighty, which was, and is, and is to come." This is to rise from prayer to worship, from supplication to adoration.

# MARCH 24

*[Abram] believed in the* LORD; *and he counted it to him for righteousness.*—Gen. 15:6

From this we must not understand that it was "Abram's faith considered by itself (if such a thing were possible, which indeed it is not, for faith cannot exist without an object; if we believe, we must believe something) that brought him the blessing." There was no merit in his faith. For that would be to make his justification to depend, in part at least, upon something in himself. Then it would not be wholly of grace, nor would his justification be secure. But in Romans 4:16 the apostle shows that it was "of faith, that it might be by grace," and this "to the end of the promise might be sure." Abram believed God up to the measure that God was pleased to reveal to him Himself and His purpose. By faith he received the blessing that God promised. He accepted it on the credit of God's word. To justify is God's part; to trust is faith's part. How far more fully God has revealed His mind and purpose to us in this our day! How much more clearly we are privileged to see the ground of our acceptance!

# MARCH 25

*I will never leave thee, nor forsake thee.*—Heb. 13:5

This was a promise given by Jehovah to more than one Old Testament saint (Gen. 28:15; Deut. 31:6, 8; Josh. 1:5; 1 Chron. 28:20). The inspired writer of the epistle to the Hebrews has no hesitation, however, in applying the words to the needs of New Testament believers.

"Be content with such things as ye have: *for he hath said.*" It is the word that Jehovah has spoken that is the sure ground for our confidence. Resting on that foundation, we may add, "So that we may boldly say, The Lord is my helper, and I will not fear what man shall do unto me."

All spiritual blessings are comprehended in that one promise. Let our faith grasp that fact. Let us not only pray, "Lord, be Thou with me"; let us rise to the apprehension of the actual present reality—"Lord, Thou *art* with me." "Yea, though I walk through the valley of the shadow of death, I will fear no evil: for thou art with me; thy rod and thy staff they comfort me" (Ps. 23:4).

# MARCH 26

*The kingdom of heaven is as a man traveling into a far country,
who called his own servants, and delivered unto them his
goods ... to every man according to his several ability.*
—Matt. 25:14, 15

The allusion to this custom between master and slaves
would be familiar to those who listened to our Lord in
those days. The parable points to the interval between our
Lord's first and second advents. It is to those who are
called "his own servants" that He entrusts His goods and
gives His charge. As all that the slave possesses belongs to
his master, so everything we have, in the way of talents or
natural gifts, as well as spiritual grace, belongs to our Lord
and Master Jesus Christ. The gifts in this parable, unlike
the parable of the pounds, are not equal. It brings out the
diversity of talent. Time is a talent. Intellectual power
is a talent. Moral capacity is a talent. Religious opportunity is a talent. Relative influence is a talent. These are
bestowed, not that we should simply keep them securely,
much less squander them, but that we should diligently use
them. Use them for God. The Lord is coming to judge us.

# MARCH 27

*To him that soweth righteousness shall be a sure reward.*
—Prov. 11:18

"The reward follows righteousness as fruit follows the seed."
This kind of sowing is never lost labor. Even in this life
we are permitted to see the result of righteous sowing. But
we can never know the *full* reward of righteousness here
on earth. It extends to the life that lies beyond the grave.
Every true act of righteousness may be looked at from
two points of view. It may be regarded as the fruit of an
inner spiritual life, of a divine principle within the man.
Or it may be looked at as the seed which is to bring forth
fruit in the lives of others. Sowing righteousness is the work
in which every soul is engaged who is living the true Christ-
life. Every such life must be productive of fruit to God.
It brings its own reward, even if we think only of the sweet
peace and joy that fills the heart of him who is thus sowing. Besides this, there is the divine approval that rests upon
the soul now, and the prospect of the Master's satisfaction
that shall be realized hereafter: "Behold, I come quickly,
and *my reward* is with me, to give to every man according
as his work shall be" (Rev. 22:12).

## MARCH 28

*Be strong and of a good courage.*—Josh. 1:18

This is not the strength of animal courage and good spirits. It is the strength that comes through faith. It is not the strength that rests on faith, but of that on which faith rests. The strength comes as faith grasps the fact revealed: "For the LORD thy God is with thee whithersoever thou goest." It is not prayer that makes this true. But it is prayer that enables us to see this truth. God declares the fact, faith accepts it, and at once all fear vanishes. Looking at the command in connection with Joshua it meant strength in the hands and firmness in the knees (Isa. 35:3; cf. Heb. 12:12, 13). The believer who knows what it is to be delivered from the bondage of Egypt, who knows what it is to come up out of the wilderness on the borders of the good land, needs this word of exhortation and command. He must be strong to go up and take possession of his inheritance. "Every place that the sole of your foot shall tread upon, that have I given unto you (Josh. 1:3).

## MARCH 29

*Come, ye blessed of my Father, inherit the kingdom prepared for you from the foundation of the world.*—Matt. 25:34

"Fear not, little flock," said our Lord, "for it is your Father's good pleasure to give you the kingdom." The kingdom is ours already, but the time will come when He will say unto us, "Come ye and *inherit* it." It is one of those things which we are told in His Word He has "prepared" for us. "Eye hath not seen, nor ear heard, neither have entered into the heart of man, the things which God hath prepared for them that love him" (1 Cor. 2:9). This does not mean they cannot yet be known by us. They are beyond our highest grasp of thought, "but God hath revealed them unto us by his Spirit."

Note especially that word *inherit*. Heaven is an inheritance. All who enter in are children. Because all God's children are heirs—heirs of God and joint-heirs with Christ. Strangers and aliens cannot inherit. If, therefore, we would be amongst those to whom these gracious words shall be addressed, we must be heirs. And to become an heir we must be *born* into God's family. Have you been born from above—born of God?

# MARCH 30

*Isaac went out to meditate in the field at the eventide.*
—Gen. 24:63

There is nothing more needed in this busy age than quiet times to be alone with God. Prayer is not the only occupation of the soul when we draw near to the throne of grace. It is not simply to make our requests known to God that we draw nigh to Him. We come to hear His voice. We come to hear His will. As we meditate on His Word we are sowing the seeds of future action. It is as we submit our hearts and minds to the truth of His Word that we become possessed by it, and conformed to the image of His Son. "Thy words were found, and I did eat them" (Jer. 15:16). It is only by quiet prayerful meditation that this spiritual assimilation takes place. Then follows what the prophet records: "And thy word was unto me the joy and rejoicing of mine heart." We cannot all go into the field like Isaac and meditate, but, as one has said, "the Lord is in the town too, and will meet with thee in thy chamber or in the crowded street. Let thy heart go forth to meet Him."

# MARCH 31

*My God shall supply all your need according to his riches in glory by Christ Jesus.*—Phil. 4:19

The apostle leads the Philippian converts at once to the fountain of all blessing. "My God"—how great and glorious and all-sufficient God was to him! It is He who shall look after them who had so lovingly been thinking of his necessities and ministering to his wants. *"All* your need," no matter how great and how varying. He shall fill them all to the full. Let your need be as the empty vessel which is brought to the fountain to be filled. The greater your need, the larger the vessel, the deeper the capacity, and the richer and fuller the blessing. And this He will do—not simply *out* of His riches or glory, but *according* to riches. The first would indicate the *source* only, but the latter shows us the *measure* of the supply. It was in dependence on such a God that the apostle lived. He spoke of himself "as having nothing, and yet possessing all things." None of God's gifts, however rich and precious, could make him for a moment independent of God. His great fullness and our emptiness have continually to meet.

# APRIL 1

*The fruit of the Spirit is . . . joy.*—Gal. 5:22

But joy does not come alone. It comes between "love" and "peace." Those are the three things we cannot bring about in ourselves by any direct efforts of our own, however earnestly we may try. We cannot make ourselves "love," or rejoice, or be peaceful. They are the fruit of the Spirit. In relation to these inner conditions of mind we are to be passive. It is the Holy Spirit who produces this fruit and fills our heart with such emotions. The active virtues follow as the necessary outcome of this inner condition. It is when divine "love, joy, and peace" are graciously filling our hearts that our actions will be characterized by long-suffering, gentleness, goodness, faithfulness, etc.

Let us recognize the Holy Spirit's personality and presence, as One dwelling within us. If we are grieving Him, how can He comfort us? He is then our Reprover. But it is emphatically His office to comfort. When we honor Him, and yield to His gracious sovereign sway, then He not only ceases to reprove—He begins at once to fill our hearts with His fruit.

# APRIL 2

*If ye do return unto the Lord with all your hearts, then put away the strange gods and Ashtaroth from among you, and prepare your hearts unto the Lord, and serve Him only.*
—1 Sam. 7:3

Samuel appeals to the people to prove the sincerity of their repentance by a practical separation from that which was the cause of their apostasy.

*"Return."* This is the first step. If there has been declension and departure, it is not to improve your condition that God bids you to take heed, but to return to Him.

*"Put away the strange gods."* We never do return to the Lord if we are not sincerely forsaking our sins. From these words of the prophet it would seem that he suspected the reality of their outward demonstrations of sorrow. He would say to them, If indeed your repentance is genuine, it will have this sure mark: your actions will be in harmony with your words. You will

*"Prepare your hearts unto the Lord."* It is with Him who searches the hidden secrets of our being that we have to do.

## APRIL 3

*Beloved, be not ignorant of this one thing, that one day is with
the Lord as a thousand years, and a thousand years as one
day. The Lord is not slack concerning his promise, as some
men count slackness.*—2 Pet. 3:8, 9

Why does God delay in fulfilling His promise? It is not
because of inability or fickleness, as is the case with men.
He delays because He is "longsuffering to us-ward, not
willing that any should perish."

"Peter views God's eternity in relation to the last day.
It seems to us, short-lived beings, long in coming; but *with
the Lord* the interval is irrespective of the idea of long or
short. His eternity exceeds all measures of time. To His
divine knowledge future things are present. His power requires not long delays for performing His work. His longsuffering excludes men's impatient expectation. He can do
the work of a thousand years in one day."

But what is the promise here referred to? It is the promise of His Coming—His Second Advent. It was at this
that men scoffed. It was so then; it is so now. But the believer expects what the Lord has promised (2 Pet. 3:13).

## APRIL 4

*Fear not; I am the first and the last.*—Rev. 1:17

"The First by Creation, the Last by retribution. First, because before Me there was no God; Last, because after
Me there shall be no other. First, because from Me are
all things; Last, because to Me all things return."

A view of the risen Lord brought the apostle to the
dust. "And when I saw him, I fell at his feet as dead."
It is thus that we learn what true humility means, and
the way by which it is brought about.

There is no better place than this—"at his feet"—to hear
His voice and to feel His hand. "He laid his right hand
upon me."

It was as the apostle lay there "as dead" that this gracious message came to him. Let us take in all the consolation this passage unfolds to us. Four things may be
noted in connection with this revelation of the risen Lord to
His servant John: What He did—"laid his right hand upon
me." What He is—"I am. . . ." What He possesses—"the
keys of hell and of death." What He commands—"Fear
not." Let the soul take a full view of the risen and exalted
Lord and Savior, and fear will vanish.

# APRIL 5

*I will not let thee go, except thou bless me.*—Gen. 32:26

Jacob had passed from the wrestling or resisting stage to the clinging stage when he said these words. It is to this stage of that memorable encounter that those words in Hosea 12:3, 4 refer: "By his strength he had power with God: Yea, he had power over the angel, and prevailed: he wept, and made supplication unto him." But this did not begin until after his power of resistance was gone. It was not until the Lord "touched the hollow of his thigh" that Jacob became a suppliant. Up to that moment he was on the defensive. Jacob was not ignorant of God. He had had a saving manifestation of Jehovah at Bethel, but although brought into the privileges of the covenant, Jacob was still a "carnal" believer (1 Cor. 3:1, 2), and much needed to be done in him before he could follow the Lord fully. This event in Jacob's history marks a second crisis in his spiritual life, as memorable as the first twenty years before. It was now that he received a new name: "Thy name shall be called no more Jacob, but Israel: for as a prince hast thou power with God and with men, and hast prevailed."

# APRIL 6

*He ever liveth to make intercession.*—Heb. 7:25

There were three great parts of the high priest's office—to atone, to make intercession, and to bless. It is as the Intercessor that Christ is here put before us. The fact that He has the "power of an endless life"—an unchangeable priesthood—that He ever lives to make intercession for us, is the reason given why "He is able to save . . . to the uttermost": that is, to the very end of time. If He ever ceased to hold the office of High Priest there might be ground to fear that it is not possible for us to continue on our way to the end. Under the old dispensation it was quite true no priest continued always to hold that office. If for no other reason, there was the fact that death, in due time, came and removed him. But here is the contrast. Christ is unlike the Aaronic priests in that respect. He is after the order of Melchisedec—a priest *for ever*. Death has no power over Him. He is therefore able to be saving all those who are in the habit of drawing nigh unto God through Him evermore—to the very end of earth's journey.

# APRIL 7

*As sorrowful, yet alway rejoicing; as poor, yet making many rich; as having nothing, and yet possessing all things.*
—2 Cor. 6:10

Is the Christian life a sad or a joyous one? In one sense it is both. The Lord Jesus was "the man of sorrows," and yet one of the most precious gifts He leaves to His people is His peace (John 14:27).

To be sorrowful and yet always rejoicing is a paradox that cannot be understood intellectually, but is perfectly intelligible when we experience it practically. There may be much around us to occasion sorrow, but if within us His peace guards the heart and mind, and His Spirit fills with love and joy and peace, the life will not be a sorrowful one. No; in spite of trying circumstances we shall then know what it is to "rejoice with joy unspeakable and full of glory" (1 Pet. 1:8).

In the same way the other two statements of this paradox may be understood. The apostle was poor, and yet he was rich; he had nothing, and yet he possessed all things. Every child of God has the same inheritance in Christ. It is as he uses what God has bestowed that he brings others into the same riches.

# APRIL 8

*In every thing ye are enriched by him.*—1 Cor. 1:5

"Chapters 12-14 will show what wealth of gifts, both of Christian knowledge and of manifestations in utterance (tongues, prophecies, doctrine), had been bestowed on this Church" *(Godet)*. The knowledge of the truth and the power of making it known were divine gifts that had been richly bestowed on the Corinthian Church.

Gifts of utterance and of intellectual perception are bestowed by God. They are a part of the enrichment that comes to the Church by Christ. They are most useful and valuable endowments in the work of the ministry. But the danger with these Greek converts was to rely on these as if they were everything. They were content to be "distinguished rather by intellectual and oratorical gifts than by seriousness of heart and conscience."

Is not this the danger to which many are exposed today? It is comforting to know that God uses those who have few gifts, but are rich in grace. Our success is not a question of natural endowments, but of spiritual power.

## APRIL 9

*Fear not: for I have redeemed thee.*—Isa. 43:1

God's blessings come to us as duties as well as privileges. It is not only as a promise, but as a command, that we learn God's mind in the matter of being delivered from fear. He who says, "Steal not," also says, "Fear not." We would shrink from breaking the first command. Shall we be less careful in obeying the second? But God gives us a reason why we need not fear. It is because we are His property. "Thou art mine." "I have redeemed thee." Israel is always regarded as a redeemed people—a people that had been delivered by *price* and by *power*. The blood of the lamb and the arm of the Lord had brought them out of Egypt. It was the Lord who had redeemed them. Let this truth quiet our fears.

Dangers and difficulties there will be, and yet the Lord bids us "fear not." It is not because the need is not great, or the enemy is not stronger, or we are not weak—all this is true. But it is because He is full of grace and all-sufficient that we may take courage and "fear not."

## APRIL 10

*I am black, but comely.*—Song of Sol. 1:5

The whole volume of spiritual truth lies rolled up in these few words. You might expand them into both the Testaments. Penitence and faith . . . condemnation and peace—God's great method with man in His everlasting covenant—it is all here, 'black, but comely.' The contrast matches with the experience of every child of God . . . the solution of the paradox is the Gospel of Christ" *(Rev. J. Vaughan).*

What we think of ourselves and what God says of us are two very different things. He sees us in His Son. With Him, and with those who are in Him, He is well pleased. But we know that in us—that is, in our flesh—dwells no good thing. The more the light shines and reveals to us ourselves, the more deeply shall we feel that the first part of the above sentence describes our true nature.

And yet we know that the second part of the same sentence is true of us also. "And thy renown went forth among the heathen for thy beauty: for it was perfect through my comeliness, which I had put upon thee, saith the Lord GOD" (Ezek. 16:14).

## APRIL 11

*In the multitude of words there wanteth not sin: but he that refraineth his lips is wise.*—Prov. 10:19

The tongue is often a source of mischief and trouble to the believer. It is as difficult to control as the thoughts. There is only one thing to be done with it. It must be yielded to the Lord. It is the most important of those members that, having at one time been in the service of Satan, must now be consecrated to Christ. Like a two-edged sword, it is a weapon that is capable of incalculable mischief when in the use of the enemy of souls, but an instrument of boundless blessing when in the power and service of the Holy Ghost.

The danger here referred to is that to which those are exposed who are given to much and heedless talk. How often those who are of ready speech have to lament over the hasty word, the exaggerated statement, the sharp and cutting expression, that "in the multitude of words" escaped their lips! The rest of faith means the calm and well-regulated mind, the loving and considerate heart, the guarded lips. This is the true wisdom, "without wrangling" (James 3:17, mg.).

## APRIL 12

*What the law could not do, in that it was weak through the flesh, God sending his own Son in the likeness of sinful flesh, and for sin, condemned sin in the flesh.*—Rom. 8:3

Godet's interpretation of this passage is: "God condemned sin, a thing which the law was powerless to accomplish." "The law would certainly condemn sin in writing, by engraving its condemnation on stone, but not by displaying this condemnation in a real human life. And yet this was the necessary condition of the destruction of the sinful tendency in mankind, and to the restoration of holiness.

"Thus the first idea of this passage has been developed: *emancipation from the law of sin.* What the law condemns was condemned in Christ, that henceforth through His Spirit the law might be fully carried out in us. No doubt the power of sin is not annihilated within, but it cannot control the active part of our being and determine the walk." There is, therefore, deliverance from sin's power and service. Accept not only complete justification through Christ's death, but also the additional privilege secured to us by that death, freedom from the law of sin.

## APRIL 13

*Honour the* LORD *with thy substance, and with the firstfruits of all thine increase.*—Prov. 3:9

Spiritual sacrifices do not exclude material offerings. It is not only our souls that God would have us put into His hand, but also our substance. This shows us what value and dignity belong to all our talents. How wonderful that God should condescend to employ these things which are so essentially of the earth, earthy, in His service and kingdom! God tells us it is possible for us to "honour" Him with our substance, with our money, our gifts, our talents. He takes note of our prosperity. He knows how we have prospered, the amount of our increase. It delights His heart and honors His name when we bring our thank offerings in token that we ascribe all our prosperity to His mercy and goodness; when we confess by our actions as well as by our lips that we believe He who is the God of our spiritual gifts is also the giver of all our temporal blessings.

## APRIL 14

*My soul shall be satisfied as with marrow and fatness; and my mouth shall praise thee with joyful lips: when I remember thee upon my bed, and meditate on thee in the night watches.*—Ps. 63:5, 6

It is one thing to find relief for the conscience; it is another thing to be "satisfied," spiritually, "as with marrow and fatness." Pardon and acceptance are not the only blessings we may know on earth. There is a fullness of grace and joy beyond the mere sense of forgiveness.

"The soul that possesses God is fed full. The satisfied soul breaks into the music of praise. This satisfaction leads to a triumphant hope" *(Dr. A. Maclaren).*

Calling to mind God's acts of goodness in the past, and meditating on what He is in the present, are among the chief occupations of the soul "in the night watches." It is in this way our faith grows and our joy deepens.

It is only God that can really satisfy the soul. The world may engage its affections and absorb its thoughts, but it cannot give real satisfaction to the heart. How personal and real God was to the psalmist!

# APRIL 15

*Their Redeemer is strong.*—Jer. 50:34

This was said of Israel in the time of their oppression, and when they felt the tyranny of those who took them into captivity. During the whole of this time it was true "their Redeemer is strong"; and yet they were miserably overcome and oppressed. But they did not have the benefit of His strength, because their heart was not right with God. We read in 2 Chron. 16:9, "The eyes of the LORD run to and fro throughout the whole earth, to shew himself strong in the behalf of them whose heart is perfect toward him." It is to *show* Himself strong. What He is in *Himself* is one thing; what He is in His *manifestation* is another. In Himself our Redeemer is strong. But He will *show forth* that strength. He will *put forth* His power on behalf of those whose heart is *whole* toward Him. (See Deut. 27:6, and compare with 2 Chron. 16:9: "perfect" in the one is the same as "whole" in the other.) This is what we need to know and experience— the power of the Lord perpetually to heal and to keep, to guard and to work. It is what the Lord Himself is ready to grant. But there are certain heart conditions to be fulfilled.

# APRIL 16

*I said in my haste, I am cut off from before thine eyes: nevertheless thou heardest the voice of my supplications when I cried unto thee.*—Ps. 31:22

When we are in trial we are often tempted to impatience; we are apt to give way to hasty words. "We generally speak amiss when we are in a hurry. Hasty words are but for a moment on the tongue, but they often lie for years on the conscience." Unbelief lies at the root of all despondency. It is at such times that we say bitter things against ourselves, and, what is far worse, we think hard thoughts against God. It is not worthy of one to whom God has revealed Himself in grace to say, "I am cut off from before thine eyes." Let all such dark thoughts be banished from our minds. "Nevertheless thou heardest the voice of my supplications when I cried unto thee." Good old Gurnall observes on those words, "It is as if He had said, when I prayed with so little faith, that I, as it were, unprayed my own prayer by concluding my case in a manner desperate; yet God pardoned my hasty spirit, and gave me that mercy which I had hardly any faith to expect."

# APRIL 17

*Whoso offereth praise glorifieth me.*—Ps. 50:23

True praise does not begin with the lips; it springs up from the heart. Praise is something to be felt, but it is also something to be offered. Praise is the best sacrifice. It is that which glorifies God. It is when we are moved with a sense of God's goodness that we begin to praise.

Many of God's children desire to live lives of praise. Often they have to lament because there is so little of joy and gladness in their lives. But what are they to do? Praise is not something that comes as the result of effort. It is not by straining and struggling that we can constrain our hearts to praise. What then shall we do? Let us be occupied with that which calls forth our praise. Let us meditate upon the marvels of His grace as they are revealed to us in His Word; believing meditation on the written Word is the way by which the Holy Spirit leads God's children literally to overflow with the spirit of praise.

The prophet Isaiah puts before us the glorious exchange that may be made by those who "mourn in Zion," the desponding and cast-down children of God (Isa. 61:3).

# APRIL 18

*I will raise them up a Prophet from among their brethren, like unto thee.*—Deut. 18:18

When God spake to the children of Israel from Sinai, the people besought Moses, "Let not God speak with us, lest we die." They all felt they could not endure direct intercourse with Him without any mediation. They implored Moses to mediate the message for them. And so he became, with God's full approval, the human medium through which the divine will was conveyed. This meant being God's *prophet*. But in this Moses was a type of One who was to come.

Christ is the Mediator between God and men. He not only reveals to us what God is, and how He has come down to us, but also what we are, and how we may draw nigh to God. He is our Prophet as well as our Redeemer. We can draw nigh to Him without fear, however sinful and ignorant we are.

This promise that God made to Moses He has fulfilled. Christ is a Prophet from among the children of men. He became a man, and in that human nature fulfilled His office as God's Prophet.

# APRIL 19

*Verily, verily, I say unto you, I am the door of the sheep.*
—John 10:7

Two doors are referred to by our Lord in this passage. First, He speaks of the door of the *Shepherd* (vv. 1-3). That is the door through which He who is the *true* Shepherd, *i.e.*, the Messiah, must enter. What was that door? It was the divinely appointed way which His Father had prefigured in the types and prophecies of the Old Testament. By fulfilling those types and doing all things "according to the Scriptures," Jesus passed through the door of the Shepherd, and thus proved Himself the true Messiah.

The second is the door of the *sheep* (v. 9). Because He has shown Himself to be the true Shepherd, He has proved Himself to be the *Door of salvation*. That is the door through which *we* have to pass in order to be saved.

The path for walk and service comes after the door has been entered. He who says, "I am the door," says also, "I am the way." The use of a door is not to look through, but to pass through. It is not a door that we reach only at death. It is close at hand to every unpardoned soul. It stands open for him to enter. It divides light from darkness, life from death.

# APRIL 20

*There shall cleave nought of the cursed thing to thine hand.*
—Deut. 13:17

Before the captivity idolatry was one of Israel's greatest dangers. Very solemn and stringent were the laws laid down against this sin. Everything that was in any way brought in contact with idolatry was regarded as polluted. It mattered not what wealth or substance it was, if it had been in any way associated with the worship of heathen gods, God declared it to be " cursed," and marked His displeasure by requiring its utter destruction.

All this has an important spiritual application. "Love not the world, neither the things that are in the world. If any man love the world, the love of the Father is not in him" (1 John 2:15). Whatever takes God's place in our hearts is an idol. Even God's blessings may become a snare to us. Things innocent in themselves, when they estrange our hearts from God, are positively sinful in their influence, and must be put away if we would walk in the freedom and purity of His salvation.

# APRIL 21

*Stand fast in the Lord.*—Phil. 4:1

It is not possible to stand fast until we have found God's foundation. Many are seeking strong faith in order to be steadfast, rather than a firm rock to which to rest their faith. We are exhorted to be steadfast in four connections.

1. *Steadfast in the faith* (1 Cor. 16:13). That is, as to the truth to be held, a revelation from God, delivered once for all to the saints. Hold it with a firm grasp.

2. *Steadfast in the liberty* (Gal. 5:1). Christ by His death gained for us this liberty. By faith we enter into it, and by faith we may continue in it. It is a freedom from sin's tyranny and dominion—a freedom from sin's service.

3. *Steadfast in Christian unity* (Phil. 1:27). The ground of this unity is the fact that we, as believers in the Lord Jesus Christ, have all been baptized into one body by one Spirit (1 Cor. 12:13). The mystical Church consists of one Head, one Body, one Life. As a result of this unity of life, we may expect to realize a unity of desire and a unity of effort.

4. *Steadfast in the Lord* (Phil. 4:1). In fidelity to Him; in fellowship with Him.

# APRIL 22

*If his offering be a burnt sacrifice of the herd, let him offer a male without blemish: he shall offer it of his own voluntary will.... And he shall put his hand upon the head of the burnt offering; and it shall be accepted for him to make atonement for him.*—Lev. 1:3, 4

The antitype of all these Levitical sacrifices is to be found, not in ourselves, but in Christ. There are many shadows, but only one Substance; there are countless types, but only one real Sacrifice. The Israelite looked forward; we look backward upon that One victim, who offered Himself without spot unto God. It was a voluntary sacrifice on His part (John 10:18). It is by faith we lay our hand on the Head of that sacrifice. By that act we have the privilege of knowing that we are completely identified with Christ in His atoning death. We have the unspeakable comfort of knowing that through that death not only are our sins put away, but we are accepted and accounted righteous in Him, who is the Lord our righteousness.

## APRIL 23

*The* LORD *was my stay.*—Ps. 18:18

It is impossible to overestimate the blessing of a restful heart. To be calm and peaceful "with sorrows surging round"; to be still, yet active, even when "by thronging duties press'd," are privileges that belong only to those who have found the soul's true Resting place. "The LORD is my rock, and my fortress, and my deliverer; my God, my strength, in whom I will trust." We cannot say "My heart is fixed" until we have found the Rock that cannot be moved. It is not the strength of our efforts to cling that is our stay, but the firmness of the Rock on which we rest. The Lord is our Stay. "Thou wilt keep him in perfect peace, whose mind is stayed on thee" (Isa. 26:3). The Scriptures teach us that God is immovable, unchanging, unfailing. The Lord is *immovable*. Of nothing here on earth can this be said. Until we have made Him our Rock we can know nothing of true abiding rest. The Lord is *unchanging*. What we find Him to be to us today He will be to us tomorrow. He is "the same yesterday, and to-day, and for ever" (Heb. 13:8). In Him is "no variation, or shadow due to change" (James 1:17, RSV).

## APRIL 24

*The* LORD *visited Sarah as he had said, and the* LORD *did unto Sarah as he had spoken.*—Gen. 21:1

Another unfolding of the divine character. It is by seeing what God *is* that faith grows. Here we see Him as gracious, faithful, and omnipotent. And what He was to Sarah He is ready to be to all those who put their trust in Him.

*Gracious,* because it was in mercy and not in judgment that He "visited" her. Some of His visitations reveal His power to condemn, His hatred of sin. But in Christ Jesus it is grace that shines out with special brightness and glory amidst all the other attributes of His character.

*Faithful.* That implies a promise given. "The Lord visited Sarah *as he had said.*" Faith's great business is to lay hold of the word that He has spoken, and to rely on that. It will have to pass through severe testing, but that only increases its strength and adds to its tenacity.

*Omnipotent.* What He had promised, He is able also to perform (Rom. 4:21). It is not with God's omnipotence in the abstract that we have to do, but with that omnipotence along the line of His revealed purposes.

# APRIL 25

*Thou shalt call his name JESUS; for he shall save his people from their sins.*—Matt. 1:21

To be saved from misery may be the first and almost the only feeling that fills the newly-awakened heart; but that, after all, is only a low motive in our desires after God. The prodigal was thinking more of his escape from his wretchedness than of the longings of his father's heart. And yet it was a true beginning of a repentant life.

Salvation from *sin* is man's great necessity. And sin, God's Word teaches us, is not merely a misfortune in relation to man, it is an offense in reference to God. To be saved from sin, therefore, something more than power is needed—worth or price is necessary in the form of a ransom. Such was the sacrifice of Christ. It was the price of our redemption. "Ye are bought with a price" (1 Cor. 6:20); redeemed, not with silver and gold, but with the precious blood of Jesus Christ (1 Pet. 1:18, 19). But if Christ's sacrifice saves us from sin's penalty, it also saves us from sin's power. It is a deliverance from the dominion of sin, from its service. This is a freedom we may know now (Luke 1:74, 75).

# APRIL 26

*His left hand is under my head, and his right hand doth embrace me.*—Song of Sol. 2:6

It is a mercy to know that, as God has provided for our unworthiness, so He has anticipated our helplessness. His righteousness completely meets our demerit, His strength our weakness. "In the Lord have I righteousness and strength." It is a blessed thing to know, when we fall, that His everlasting arms are beneath us—ready to sustain, ready to restore. But it is a still more blessed thing to see that, because His hand is under us, *we need not fall;* because His mighty arm is outstretched on our behalf, *we need not sink.* If, as we look back to the time when He brought us up out of "the horrible pit," we see that He is "Almighty to save"—so we may know, as in the midst of manifold temptations He makes us "more than conquerors," that He is also "Almighty to keep." "Fear thou not; for I am with thee: be not dismayed; for I am thy God: I will strengthen thee; yea, I will help thee; yea, I will uphold thee with the right hand of my righteousness" (Isa. 41:10).

# APRIL 27

*Brethren, the time is short.*—1 Cor. 7:29

That is, the time is contracted, limited. There is none to waste. Every moment is needed for the work to be done. To the true disciple who would walk as his Master walked, every hour has its work and every work its appointed hour. He who gives to every man his work has allotted to each work its time. The message speaks of *opportunity*. This is one of God's gifts—the opportunity to use the grace He has bestowed for use. The time has been shortened; this reminds us of the folly of making this world our home. It bids us sit loosely to all earthly things. Their temporary character is to be remembered in all our relations to them. The apostle refers here especially to our social relations. Solemn and searching as are his precepts, let us observe there is no asceticism in his teaching, here or elsewhere. While loving husband and wife, we are not to forget that the time is short. And so with sorrow and joy, with earthly possessions and the use of this world, the same principle must run through all our relationships; the same great fact must ever be kept in view—everything here is transitory—"The time is short."

# APRIL 28

*Behold the Lamb of God.*—John 1:29

This was John the Baptist's first testimony to his disciples when he saw Jesus coming to him. It is the first view of Christ that the sin-burdened soul needs. Christ the Sin-bearer must be seen before Christ as God's ideal of holiness can be followed. He is the Lamb of God bearing away the sin of the world. "The LORD hath laid on him the iniquity of us all" (Isa. 53:6). There we see Him doing the Father's will in putting away sin by the sacrifice of Himself (Heb. 9:26). "Lo, I come to do thy will, O God" (Heb. 10:9). "By the which will we are sanctified through the offering of the body of Jesus Christ once for all" (v. 10). In that death we see God's will fulfilled, the world's sin atoned for, and the power of Satan overthrown.

This was no afterthought in the scheme of redemption. For He is the Lamb slain before the foundation of the world (Rev. 13:8).

Behold Him! There is life in a look at the Crucified One. Adore Him!

## APRIL 29

*Consider how great things he hath done for you.*—1 Sam. 12: 24

A consideration of God's past mercies strengthens our faith in His future blessings, and deepens our sense of unworthiness. We lose much from a lack of thoughtful consideration. The remembrance of what He has already done for us, and prayerful meditation thereon will dispel our doubts and turn our days of clouds and darkness into sunshine. There is divine logic in the reasoning: "He that spared not his own Son, but delivered him up for us all, how shall he not with him also freely give us all things?" (Rom. 8:32).

It is impossible to grasp the extent or to estimate the value of those gifts God has already bestowed, but we may "consider" them. Let us cultivate this habit of holy and devout meditation on the "great things" that God hath done for us. It will deepen our thankfulness and quicken the spirit of prayer. "Bless the LORD, O my soul; and *forget not* all his benefits" (Ps. 103:2).


## APRIL 30

*Whoso keepeth his Word, in him verily is the love of God perfected.*—1 John 2:5

"The phrase expresses not only the fulfillment of specific injunctions ('Keep His commandments,' verse 3), but also the needful regard to the whole revelation made by Christ as a living and active power, of which the voice is never silent. The unity of the many 'commandments' is not in a 'law,' but in a 'word'; it answers to the spirit, and not to the letter. Compare John 8:51 f., 55; 14:23; 15:20; 17:6. The passage John 14:21-24 is of singular interest as illustrating the full meaning of the phrase" *(Bishop Westcott).*

The main thought is, that the word is His word, the word of God. There is emphasis also on the 'keeping' " *(ibid.).* "St. John does not say of him (verse 4) that 'he is true, and the truth is in him'; but he rather regards his character from the divine side, and points out, not what such a man is, but what such a man has received from Him who is unchangeable. *In this man the love of God hath been perfected.*"

# MAY 1

*The fruit of the Spirit is . . . peace.*—Gal. 5:22

The first point that we should clearly see in this sentence
is this, that the Spirit here is not our new nature, which
is spirit, but the Holy Ghost Himself. All real fruit comes
directly from Him. It is not the fruit of the Christian,
but the fruit of the Spirit. Fruit *unto* the Lord is first of
all fruit *from* the Lord. But as the root needs the branches
to bear that which it produces, so the Holy Ghost takes
us into union with Himself in order that we might bear
the fruit that He brings forth.

The Holy Ghost works upon the unsaved, and produces wonderful results, even where there is no union.
But fruit implies vital union. Fruit is the outcome of the
Holy Spirit's indwelling. It implies that our spiritual being
has been brought into organic union with the living God.

Nine things are mentioned in that list that comprise
"the fruit of the Spirit." They together form one fruit.
"Peace" is closely associated with "love" and "joy." Those
three things fill the heart when the Holy Ghost is glorified
in us, and when He is about to make us fruitful branches.

# MAY 2

*Surely the* LORD *is in this place; and I knew it not.* —Gen. 28:16

The manifested presence of God makes every place a
Bethel. Sometimes we fancy if we could change our circumstances we should become more spiritual. We think it
is the place that makes the difference. But we are always
on holy ground if we are habitually living in the presence
of God. God is always with His people, but how often
they know it not! It is for us by faith to recognize His
presence. "Surely the LORD is in this place." When we
say He is present with us by faith, we must not suppose
that we have to think of Him as present—in other words,
that His presence is, first of all, to be a matter of *fancy*—
and then it will become to us a matter of fact. No, fancy
is not faith. Faith has no real existence if there is no
antecedent fact for it to rest on. "I am with you alway"
is a perpetual fact that precedes our faith. Spiritually to
apprehend that fact is not to make it true, but to grasp
that which was true before we grasped it. It is then that
fact passes into experience. For Christ is to us practically
what He is to our faith.

# MAY 3

*Be ye therefore perfect, even as your Father which is in heaven is perfect.*—Matt. 5:48

The context shows us that the main thought of the passage is "love." And love, Paul tells us, is the fulfilling of the law. It is that that gives completeness to the Christian character. To be perfected in love is to find our dwelling place in God, who is Love. The words occur in our Lord's Sermon on the Mount. "The Sermon on the Mount differs from all contemporary Jewish teaching; so also is it impossible to compare it with any other system of morality. The difference here is one, not of degree, nor even of kind, but of standpoint." "Every moral system is a road by which, through self-denial, discipline, and effort, men seek to reach the goal. *Christ begins with this goal,* and places His disciples at once in the position to which all other teachers point as the end. They work up to the goal of becoming the 'children of the Kingdom'; He makes men such, freely, and of His grace; and this *is* the Kingdom. What the others labour for, He gives. They begin by demanding, He by bestowing; because He brings good tidings of forgiveness and mercy" *(Dr. Edersheim).*

# MAY 4

*Behold, the Lord's hand is not shortened, that it cannot save; neither his ear heavy, that it cannot hear.*—Isa. 59:1

It was Israel's sins and iniquities that had compelled the Lord not to hear, as we read in the following verse. It was not that His power was insufficient, or that He was ignorant of their deep need and distress. God cannot hear prayers that are not sincere—not from the heart, however regularly they may be uttered. The question may be asked today, How comes it to pass that the Lord's people are often in such distress? How can we account for the fact that the cause of Christ makes such slow progress? Where is the Lord God of Israel? Has the Spirit of God ceased to work in the midst of His people? The answer is to be sought, not in any supposed change in the character of Jehovah or in the failure of His strength: it is to be found in the impenitence of His people; in their lack of humiliation and contrition. "Your sins have hid his face"; literally, "Your sins have caused His face to be hidden from you." The way of power is through confession of sin and its renunciation.

# MAY 5

*Take no thought, saying, What shall we eat? or, What shall we drink? or Wherewithal shall we be clothed? ... For your heavenly Father knoweth that ye have need of all these things.*—Matt. 6:31, 32

It is against anxious thought that our Lord here warns His hearers. There is nothing in these words to encourage the careless neglect of means. It is concerning unbelieving anxiety that He speaks. It was no doubt the besetting sin of many in those days, as it is now, to worry and to fret in reference to the things that perish. The same questions they asked then are absorbing the minds of multitudes today, as if a man's life consisted in the abundance of the things that he possessed.

One secret of freedom from these anxious thoughts is in the fact that our heavenly Father knows all about us— knows exactly what we really need.

The other is found in following the divine direction, "Seek ye *first* the kingdom of God, and his righteousness; and all these things shall be added unto you" (Matt. 6:33).

# MAY 6

*Mercy and truth are met together; righteousness and peace have kissed each other.*—Ps. 85:10

God's glory is seen in the manifestation of His attributes. And the "glory of God in the face of Jesus Christ" consists chiefly in the union of those attributes. All are magnified. Not one is sacrificed. It is only at the cross we see "mercy and truth" meeting together; "righteousness and peace" kissing each other. It is only there we see how God can be just, and yet the justifier of the ungodly. (Compare Rom. 3:26 with 4:5.)

We have not found the true foundation until we see that we depend as much upon the justice and faithfulness of God as upon His mercy and compassion. "If we confess our sins, he is faithful and just to forgive us our sins, and to cleanse us from all unrighteousness" (1 John 1:9).

He is faithful to the terms of the eternal covenant between Himself and His Son; He is just to Him who, according to the terms of that covenant, undertook to die in the place of those who should confess their sins.

# MAY 7

*Ye shall hear of wars and rumours of wars: see that ye be not troubled.*—Matt. 24:6

Our Lord's exhortations to restful confidence were given with the clearest prevision of all the troubles and trials that were about to come upon His Church. He knew it would be a time of fierce persecution, and yet He could say, with the certain knowledge that they were not empty words, "See that ye be not troubled." He knew that a new power was about to take possession of His people, that could make them "patient in tribulation," and that would enable them to "rejoice with joy unspeakable and full of glory," even in days of darkest trial.

"Let not your heart be troubled: ye believe in God, believe also in me" (John 14:1). "Let your faith find in *Me* One on whom it can rest. In Christ, belief in God gained a present reality. The simultaneous injunction of faith in God, and in Christ, under the same conditions, implies the divinity of Christ. The belief is 'in Christ,' and not in any propositions about Christ." Here is the secret of freedom from trouble (Ps. 112:7).

# MAY 8

*It pleased the LORD to bruise him; he hath put him to grief.*—Isa. 53:10

Peter declared on the day of Pentecost that Christ had been "delivered by the determinate counsel and foreknowledge of God" (Acts 2:23). The unjust deeds of men were permitted by God, to carry out and accomplish His own predetermined counsel.

It is a thought full of encouragement, as the sinner draws nigh to the cross, burdened with guilt, that here is *God's* way of atonement—God's way of deliverance from the penalty of sin. It is not an experiment, devised by human devotion, by which to propitiate God. It is *God* who "hath laid upon him the iniquity of us all." Both the Father and the Son are of one mind in this wondrous transaction. It was the Father's good pleasure that the Son should die, "the just for the unjust." And it was the Son's own voluntary act, to lay down His life as a sacrifice for sins. The whole work is divine. The sinner need not hesitate to roll his burden off on Him who is the divinely-appointed Sinbearer.

## MAY 9

*Faith is the substance of things hoped for, the evidence of
  things not seen.*—Heb. 11:1

If this may be called a definition, it is the only definition
of faith we have in the Bible. Before he gives us its working, and its results in the lives of men, the inspired writer
puts before us its nature. He thus describes it: "Faith is
the substance [or confidence] of things hoped for." It sub-
stantiates the *promises* of God; and not the promises only,
but the *present facts* or realities of revelation, which are
to sight, for the most part, unseen. What we cannot see
with the natural eye, what we cannot touch and realize
with physical sense, faith enables us to grasp as actually
present and true. Faith must not be confounded with
fancy. God does not say, *"Imagine* these blessings in your
heart, and believe them, *as if* they were really true." No;
God begins by declaring their actual existence, that they
are already true, and *because* they are true, commands
us to believe. He never bids us believe without providing a
foundation of *promise* or of *fact* on which to rest our
faith. And so faith becomes to us "the evidence" or dem-
onstration—the convincing proof—of things not seen.

## MAY 10

*For this purpose the Son of God was manifested, that he might
  destroy the works of the devil.*—1 John 3:8

The manifestation of Christ as the sacrifice for sin, as
the Savior of the world, has more than one purpose to
accomplish. It may be said with truth, "For this purpose
the Son of God was manifested, that He might reveal
God's love to men—that He might draw all men unto
Himself." But here another aspect of the divine purpose
is set forth: "That he might destroy the works of the
devil." The fulfillment of that purpose is both present and
future. There are benefits of Christ's death that bear on
the immediate present. For this purpose the Son of God
was manifested, that we might be delivered now, in this
life, from the pursuit of sin in every form—that we might
be set free from doing "the works of the devil."

But there are other "works of the devil" it was Christ's
purpose to destroy. Such, for instance, as all his efforts
to deceive—his "wiles"—his allurements and temptations.
Deliverance from these belongs to the future.

## MAY 11

*Awake to righteousness, and sin not.*—1 Cor. 15:34

It is from a condition of moral insensibility that we are aroused to a life of practical righteousness. Our spiritual enemy would never disturb souls that are wrapped in this state of slumber. While in that sleep we have no concern either for our own soul or for the souls of others. But more than this: as in natural sleep, so in moral slumber, often our minds are filled with fancies. We dream of possessions that do not exist; we live on delusions, and waste our time on fictions. The Gospel is a summons from this state of insensibility and delusion to a life of reality and a walk of righteousness. It is not the sinner alone who needs the call. The Church herself needs it. We too, as individual believers, need to arise and shake ourselves from the dust. "Awake, thou that sleepest, and arise from the dead"—i.e., from among those who are dead in trespasses and sins—"and Christ shall give thee light" (Eph. 5:14). Thou hast received His life, but thou hast been sleeping amongst the dead, identifying thyself with the world. "Awake!" and He who has given life will give *light*.

## MAY 12

*Beloved, let us love one another: for love is of God; and every one that loveth is born of God, and knoweth God.*—1 John 4:7

Life, light, and love are the three great topics on which the Apostle John delights to dwell. The embodiment of each, he declares, is found in God Himself. It is those who, having received the *life,* and are now called to walk in the *light,* that may know the still higher lesson of *love*. "Love is of God, and therefore, since it proceeds from Him, it must be the characteristic also of those who partake in His nature, as His children" *(Westcott)*.

Love is regarded by the apostle as the region of action; just as truth is referred to as the region of thought. The believer's true home is the love of God—or in God, who is Love. "To abide in love is to abide in the thoughts of God's love, in the memory and consciousness of Christ's love, in the sense of one's own unworthiness, and in the renunciation of self . . . in intercession, in the Holy Spirit, in the faith that discerns a present God, and knows how to discover the relations of every creature to God" *(George Bowen)*

# MAY 13

*Pray every where, lifting up holy hands, without wrath and doubting.*—1 Tim. 2:8

The words remind us of Solomon at the dedication of the Temple. He "stood before the altar of the LORD in the presence of all the congregation of Israel, and spread forth his hands toward heaven" (1 Kings 8:22). David says in Ps. 141:2, "Let my prayer be set forth before thee as incense; and the lifting up of my hands as the evening sacrifice." It was the custom in primitive times for Christians, in craving for divine help, to turn up the palms of their hands towards heaven. *"Holy* hands" means hands that are sanctified to God—yielded up, set apart to Him for a holy use. These "instruments" that were once yielded to sin are now consecrated to God. The apostle's desire was that the followers of Jesus Christ should be men of real prayer. *Everywhere* the breath of fervent supplication could ascend to God—"without wrath and doubting." These will sadly mar our prayers. Few things are more common, even amongst Christians, than an unforgiving spirit. Nothing will more effectually rob our souls of spiritual power than a feeling of malice and the habit of carnal reasoning.

# MAY 14

*The fellowship of his sufferings.*—Phil. 3:10

The condition of knowing Christ and the power of His resurrection is here stated. It is "being made comfortable unto his death." There is a close connection between "the fellowship of his sufferings" and conformity to His death. It was this that took place at the apostle's conversion. He counted all things but loss in order that he might know Christ; and to know Him not only in the atoning efficacy of His death, but in the power of His resurrection. This necessitated a complete identification of himself with Christ in that death. And so it must be with the believer, even after the great transition from death to life has taken place. There is a deeper and a truer knowledge of Him and the power of His resurrection. This can come only with a fuller and more complete identification with Him in His death. Fellowship implies union; but it is more than union—it is participation. There is a sense in which Christ died alone. He bore the burden of human guilt. He alone atoned for sin. It is also true that we died *with* Him.

# MAY 15

*God shall wipe away all tears . . . there shall be no more death, neither sorrow . . . for the former things are passed away.*
—Rev. 21:4

Instead of "all tears," we should translate "every tear," and so possess the promise in its true and tender form. The first, or former, things are passed away: "Death shall not be any longer; neither shall mourning, nor crying, nor pain be any longer. . . . The splendid array of negatives come as heralds of the positive peace of the New Jerusalem: no sin, no tears, no death, no mourning, no crying, no pain; with the former things these six shadows pass away from life" *(Bishop Ellicott's Commentary).*

The time here referred to is not the millennium; for in the millennium there will be death. It points to a period that shall follow the thousand years of Christ's reign upon earth (Isa. 65:20; 1 Cor. 15:26, 54).

But there is a rest from sorrow and a joy in pain, to be known before we can reach this state of perfect blessedness.

# MAY 16

*A servant of Jesus Christ.*—Rom. 1:1

The word servant suggests the idea of a master and of a service. The highest title that is known in earth or heaven is "a servant of God." Now the apostles used the phrases "a servant of God" and "a servant of Christ" indiscriminately, as if they were exactly synonymous. This shows us indirectly Christ's essential deity. In the passage before us Paul places the title of servant before that of apostle because he regarded it as the higher of the two: "Paul, a servant of Jesus Christ, called to be an apostle, separated unto the gospel of God." Then let us never forget it was one of our blessed Lord's own titles. He was emphatically God's Servant: "Behold my servant, whom I uphold; mine elect, in whom my soul delighteth" (Isa. 42:1). The true servant is the one who is wholly yielded to his Master's will, whose joy consists in doing his Master's pleasure. Then it is we learn what is meant by the words, "Whose service is perfect freedom." Servitude is bondage, but the service of Christ is the liberty of love. When we love what God commands, then we find that none of His commands are grievous.

# MAY 17

*I am the* Lord *your God; walk in my statutes, and keep my judgments, and do them.*—Ezek. 20:19

God not only declares to us His requirement, He reveals to us His relationship. In that requirement we see what He expects of us, and in that relationship we see what He provides for us. "Give what Thou commandest," said Augustine, "and then command what Thou wilt." It is when we lose sight of God—what He is, not merely in Himself, or in the abstract, but what He is to us—that we get into bondage and difficulty. The command, "Walk in my statutes, and keep my judgments, and do them," alone will soon fill us with despair. But when we know that the Lord is our God—that it is God who is "at work in you, both to will and to work for his good pleasure" (Phil. 2:12, RSV)—then we see we need not faint, we need not give way to discouragement. God undertakes, when we yield ourselves wholly to Him and trust Him fully, to accomplish in us and through us that which He requires of us. The holiness which is *to* the Lord is a holiness which is first *from* the Lord.

# MAY 18

*As the Father hath life in himself; so hath he given to the Son to have life in himself.*—John 5:26

"The Son has not life only as given, but life *in Himself* as being a spring of life" *(Bishop Westcott).*

"To have life in himself, just as the Father has it in Himself, and to be an independent source of life to others, cannot be said of any creature or mere man. We all live and move and have our being in God, and are absolutely depending on Him" *(Lange).*

But "it pleased the Father that in him should all fulness dwell." This is represented as being the appointment of the Father. Christ is the Fountain of life. It is to Him we draw nigh if we would partake of that life. "In him was life," says the Apostle John (John 1:4). It is in Him as it is in God. And so He could say not only, "I am the way, the truth"—but also "the *life.*"

It is only as we know Him and receive Him that we have life. "He that hath the Son hath life." The gift of life is bound up in the gift of the Son Himself.

But there is not only life, but abundance of life, in Him.

## MAY 19

*Wash me thoroughly from mine iniquity.*—Ps. 51:2

Dr. Kay says: "The word here is used of washing a *garment*. The stain had penetrated into the very texture of his conscience." David is thinking of something more than pardon. No one knew better than he did the preciousness of divine forgiveness. But to have sins blotted out of God's book was not all that he sought. He desired that the defilement which the transgression had brought with it should be cleansed away. He therefore prays, not for pardon only, but for purification. "If we confess our sins, he is faithful and just to *forgive* us our sins, and to *cleanse* us from all unrighteousness" (1 John 1:9).

There are some who ask for pardon who do not really seek forgiveness of sins as much as they desire deliverance from sin's consequences. They want to be saved from the penalty of sin, but they have no real desire to be freed from its guilt. The soul that really seeks God's forgiveness longs as much for purity as for pardon. He is not content to have his transgressions blotted out and forgotten—he desires to be purified from sin's pollution.

## MAY 20

*Take heed unto thyself.*—1 Tim. 4:16

Two things are of the first importance—the doctrine we hold and the life we live. The apostle recognizes the necessity of taking heed to each. "Take heed unto thyself, and unto the doctrine."

It is not enough to make sure that our views are scriptural and our doctrines sound. We must be sound "in charity, in patience," and in practice.

To take heed to oneself does not mean that we should encourage ourselves in the habit of introspection. It means that a spirit of prayer and watchfulness is necessary. It means that health of soul is as essential to the spiritual life as health of body is to the natural life. There is such a thing as "getting below par," as to our physical condition. It is when we sink down into a low state of body that we are the most susceptible of disease. We then possess but little power of resistance. How true this is spiritually! Holding a sound doctrine will not compensate for living, active faith on the Lord's word, and prompt obedience to the Lord's will. Where health of soul is wanting, every spiritual faculty is affected.

## MAY 21

*My brethren, be strong in the Lord, and in the power of his might.*—Eph. 6:10

The context teaches us that the words have reference to Christian conflict; to Christian conflict in relation to our great adversary, Satan, and "spiritual wickedness in high places." These words point to that step which is preliminary to successful warfare. Before the foe can be encountered the *right position* must be taken. We must be entrenched in the strength of the Lord. We must be enclosed "in the power of his might," or, as one has paraphrased it, "in the energy of Him, the strong." It is in vain we engage in the conflict if that preliminary condition has not been fulfilled. In earthly warfare the soldier does not provide his own means of defense or weapons of assault. So in Christian conflict our whole equipment is divinely provided for us. He gives us a position that is impregnable—strength in the Lord; an armor that is impenetrable, and a weapon that is infallible—"the sword of the Spirit." We have by faith to take that position and continually to abide in it. We have by faith to put on that armor and wear it constantly.

## MAY 22

*Peace I leave with you; my peace I give unto you: not as the world giveth, give I unto you.*—John 14:27

There is the peace of reconciliation with God, and the peace of inward serenity—peace with God, and the peace of God. The Lord Jesus was referring, it would seem, to the latter, but we know from other parts of God's Word that this peace is based upon the former. We must first of all know the peace of reconciliation; then we shall be ready to receive the peace of inward repose of which our Lord speaks in these words. This is His legacy, "a legacy derived from His own treasury: *My peace.*"

In times of trial and suffering, of darkness and temptation, nothing is more essential than an inward stillness and rest of soul. This can be known only as the peace of God garrisons the heart. This it is which, like ballast in the ship, keeps our minds steady and restful amidst the storm and tumult of outward commotion. Let us note that it is Christ's own *gift* to His people. "Not as the world giveth, give I unto you." As Godet says, place the contrast on the verb *give,* and not on its object."

## MAY 23

*Thou shalt put the two stones upon the shoulders of the ephod for stones of memorial unto the children of Israel: and Aaron shall bear their names before the* LORD.—Exod. 28:12

Precious stones which should serve to remind God that the high priest represented the twelve tribes. It is rather "stones of memorial *for* the children of Israel." The high priest, when thus attired, entered the sanctuary and presented before God the whole of the children of Israel. Now we are distinctly told in Hebrews 9:9-12 that this presentation was a type or figure of that far more excellent and precious presentation which Christ is ever making of the Church before God in heaven itself. Christ *for* us is a truth that needs to be set forth with special clearness, and to be insisted upon continually, especially in these days, when the other side—Christ *in* us—is being emphasized with such power. Each has its place. To hold the one without the other is to represent a mutilated Gospel, a deformed Christianity. Christ *in* us will be a truth all the more potent and influential in proportion as the foundation truth, Christ *for* us, is laid deep and broad in our spiritual apprehension and affections.

## MAY 24

*Grieve not the holy Spirit of God, whereby ye are sealed unto the day of redemption.*—Eph. 4:30

This is one of the many passages of Scripture that point to the distinct personality of the Holy Ghost. He is not a mere quality in the divine nature, an emanation from God; He is a Person. An influence may be checked, but not "grieved." None can be grieved but one that has understanding, and will, and affections. All these are asserted of the Spirit of God. That which proves the Father and the Son to be distinct Persons is equally true of the Holy Ghost. The Holy Spirit is said to rule in and over the Church, to choose and appoint overseers, to discern and judge all things; to convince, to comfort, and to strengthen. It was as a Person our Lord spoke of Him: "I will send *him* unto you." We should mark the particular title that belongs to Him—"The *holy* Spirit of God." As such He comes to dwell in our hearts. It is by virtue of His Presence that the temple in which He dwells is also holy. "Ye are the temple of God"; "Your body is the temple of the Holy Ghost" (1 Cor. 3:16 and 6:19).

## MAY 25

*How great is thy goodness, which thou hast laid up for them that fear thee.*—Ps. 31:19

There is goodness laid up at God's right hand, that we shall know only when we enter into glory. And there is goodness laid up which we may know and experience on our way there. It is to the latter we believe the words refer. Goodness for those who fear God. Goodness to be realized by those who are willing and obedient in the day of His power: to those who walk uprightly. While it is perfectly true we are called to accept the blessings of the Gospel—a full and present pardon and a perfect righteousness—without any preliminary qualification in the way of personal merit, it is also true there are privileges that belong to the saved, which only those who walk with God and abide in Him can know in reality and in truth here on earth. How great are those privileges, how unspeakable are those blessings, of peace and joy, of liberty and triumph, of divine fellowship and fruitfulness, that are stored up in Christ for our enjoyment and equipment on our journey heavenward! "No good thing will he withhold from them that walk uprightly" (Ps. 84:11).

## MAY 26

*Our Lord Jesus, that great shepherd of the sheep.*—Heb. 13:20

This title of Shepherd, which belongs to our blessed Lord, is put before us in the Scriptures in three distinct connections—in connection with His death, His resurrection, and His Second Advent. In connection with His *death* we read, "I am the good shepherd: the good shepherd giveth his life for the sheep" (John 10:11). In connection with *resurrection,* in the passage before us, we read, "Now the God of peace, that brought again from the dead our Lord Jesus, that great Shepherd of the sheep," etc. And in connection with His *Second Coming,* "And when the chief Shepherd shall appear, ye shall receive a crown of glory that fadeth not away" (1 Pet. 5:4).

He who laid down His life for us has also given His life to us. As the risen Lord He leads His flock.

"I am the good shepherd, and know my sheep" (John 10:14). "There is a close relation," says Professor Godet, "between the verb *I know* and the possessive *My* sheep. But this knowledge is mutual."

## MAY 27

*The LORD is good, a stronghold in the day of trouble; and he knoweth them that trust in him.*—Nah. 1:7

These words occur in the midst of a description of the terrible majesty of God. They set forth His *goodness* to His people. They declare what He is to them "in the day of trouble." He is a stronghold to them at such a time. "The name of the LORD is a strong tower: the righteous runneth into it, and is safe" (Prov. 18:10). "Them that trust in him," taken literally, means "take shelter or refuge in Him." Scholars point out that the words in the original express that which is habitual and permanent. It is their wont to put their trust in the Lord and to abide under the shadow of the Almighty. Days of trouble often are turned into days of blessing, because they teach us what God can be to us in a way that days of ease or prosperity could not reveal. "The LORD knoweth them that trust in him." Not a single act of child-like faith, however secret, escapes His holy eye. He knows each trustful gaze, each step of faith, each act of confidence we repose in Him.

## MAY 28

*We look for the Saviour.*—Phil. 3:20

According to the RSV, "we await a Saviour." "The form of the verb implies a waiting full of attention, perseverance, and desire" *(Bishop Moule)*. We are looking for Him out of heaven—waiting for Him as the Savior in the full and complete sense. Now we have the salvation of our souls. But when He shall come He "shall change the body of our humiliation, that it may be conformed to the body of His glory." He shall save us then from the very presence of sin, and from temptation and sorrow and pain. The return of the Lord and Savior Jesus Christ is *the* hope of the waiting Church. The salvation for which we wait is emphatically that of the body (Rom. 8:23). "To the ancient philosopher the body was merely the prison of the spirit; to the Apostle, it is its counterpart, destined to share with it, in profound harmony, the coming heaven" *(Bishop Moule* on the Epistle to the Philippians). Let this be the attitude of the soul each day: "Looking for that blessed hope, and the glorious appearing of the great God and our Saviour Jesus Christ" (Titus 2:13).

# MAY 29

*The life of the flesh is in the blood: and I have given it to you upon the altar to make an atonement for your souls: for it is the blood that maketh an atonement for the soul.*
—Lev. 17:11

The blood is the vehicle of life; literally, it is "the soul of the flesh is in the blood." And "the blood maketh atonement by means of the soul." The life is in the blood; and so long as the blood is circulating through the body, the body lives. But when the blood is poured out, what we have then is not life, but *death*. So that *shed blood is equivalent to death*. Now, it is important to remember that always in the New Testament, where the blood of Jesus is referred to, it is blood as shed; and therefore, in every place, it is not the life of the Lord Jesus that is contemplated, but His *death*. When we commemorate His atoning sacrifice at the Lord's Supper, we do show forth, not His life, but His *death* (1 Cor. 11:26). Identification with that death, sympathy and union of heart and will with that death, which was a death unto sin, is one of the best means of bearing about in the body the putting to death of the Lord Jesus (2 Cor. 4:10).

# MAY 30

*Let us labour therefore to enter into that rest.*—Heb. 4:11

The danger of the Hebrew believer, who did not reject Jesus of Nazareth, but received Him as the Messiah, was that of coming short of the *present* privileges that belonged to him as a Christian (Heb. 4:1). There were many blessings they were in danger of missing, simply by supposing that they could not be realized in this life. Among other privileges was that of rest—the rest of God —"His rest." This was one of the blessings that *remained* to them as unappropriated by them. It was typified in Canaan (Num. 14:30; Heb. 3:18, 19; 4:8). It was spoken of by David (Heb. 4:7; Ps. 95:7). It was "promised" to them in the Old Testament (Heb. 4:1). And it "remained" to them in the Gospel (Heb. 4:9). They did not have to wait for it until they reached heaven. We are privileged to enter into this "sabbath rest" now. It is a mistake to suppose that the words point to the rest of heaven. It is a rest we enter into *by faith*—and now. Here is the secret of all true service, of all effective labor and activity.

# MAY 31

*Thy name shall be called no more Jacob, but Israel: for as a prince hast thou power with God and with men, and hast prevailed.*—Gen. 32:28

The incident to which these words refer is often spoken of as a remarkable illustration of the power of prayer. Wrestling Jacob is held up as the great example of prevailing prayer. But if the incident is an illustration of importunate supplication in its closing scene, it is certainly a striking example of human resistance to the divine will, and of obstinate self-will, in the first part of the encounter. God withstood Jacob, and Jacob resisted God. That is the first phase of the conflict. It is precisely what takes place today in countless instances where God's children, in spite of many mercies and divine longsuffering, continue to pursue a life of self-seeking and carnal policy and of resistance to the will of God. The crisis came when God "touched the hollow of his thigh." Instantly his power of resistance was gone, and he could *wrestle* no longer. *Wrestling* Jacob became *clinging* Jacob. This was the power that prevailed with God. "By his strength he had power with God: yea, he had power over the angel and prevailed."

# JUNE 1

*The fruit of the Spirt is . . . longsuffering, gentleness.*
—Gal. 5:22

If "love, joy," and "peace" describe the inner condition, "longsuffering, gentleness, goodness," would seem to point to the outward conduct. " 'Longsuffering' is *passive,* 'patient endurance under injuries inflicted by others'; 'gentleness' is *neutral,* a 'kindly disposition toward one's neighbours,' not necessarily taking a practical form; 'goodness' is *active* as an energetic principle" *(Bishop Lightfoot).*

We must not confound "longsuffering" with a dogged endurance, which is often the result of indifference and obstinacy, and in which there is neither meekness nor love. Nor, again, is "gentleness" to be confounded with an easy-going disposition which lacks decision and strength of character. "Gentleness," which is the fruit of the Holy Ghost, has nothing of timidity in it. Some of the most courageous spirits have been remarkable for their gentleness. But these are not virtues to be manufactured by the Christian. They are fruit to be brought forth by the Spirit. The Christian is as a *branch,* and not the *root.*

## JUNE 2

*Thus shall ye eat it; with your loins girded, and ye shall eat it in haste: it is the LORD's passover.*—Exod. 12:11

"It is the LORD's passover." These are very emphatic words. They seem to say, "This is no common meal; it is not even an ordinary sacrificial repast. The lamb is Jehovah's. It is His pass-sign—the mark of His protection—the means of your preservation. In this light then regard it, and though ye eat it in haste, eat it with reverence." And if this is true of the type, what shall we say of the Anti-type? With what solemn thankfulness and devout reverence should we contemplate that sacrifice of which the Lord's Supper is a commemoration and a sign! The passover was a feast for the Lord's people who were under the shelter of the blood. So the Lord's Supper is a feast intended for those who are covered by the atoning merits of Jesus Christ. We have to remember, too, that as yet we are but pilgrims; and so we have to eat it with our loins girded, and in an attitude of readiness for the Master's summons. The passover was a feast that looked forward to the true Lamb of God. The Lord's Supper is a feast that looks back to the same great central fact.

## JUNE 3

*Watch therefore, for ye know neither the day nor the hour wherein the Son of man cometh.*—Matt. 25:13

"I remember," says a well-known writer, "once living at a place where a large number of people were constantly employed in keeping the walks, grounds, and gardens in order. The proprietor was absent, and everything had a sleepy, slovenly look. But when tidings came that he would soon return, all became awake, earnest, and active. The pruning, the rolling, the weeding, the sweeping, went on amain; none rested till all was ready; and all were gratified by the look and word of approval, when the master came." And so, if we constantly remembered the words, "Ye know neither the day nor the hour wherein the Son of man cometh," we should feel it is not the time to sleep. It is a time for watchfulness, for earnest diligence and unceasing activity. The time is short, and the day of the Lord's return is close at hand. "What I say unto you," said our Lord to His disciples, "I say unto all, Watch" (Mark 13:37). The disciple who lives in the spirit of watchfulness will meditate on his Master's word, will live in the Master's presence . . . doing his Master's will.

# JUNE 4

*The glory of this latter house shall be greater than of the former . . . and in this place will I give peace.*—Hag. 2:9

The second Temple was not greater in architectural splendor, but in the fact that the glory of the Messiah was there. The first Temple was burned by the Chaldees, the wall of Jerusalem was broken down, and the people carried captive to Babylon, and it was more than fifty years after that the foundation of the second house was laid. Jehovah would not manifest Himself in the same degree as He had before, to a people who were suffering the chastisement of their backslidings; and the house they had built Him was but a poor copy of the Temple that had perished. Yet it was this that the Lord promised through His servant the prophet, that this second Temple in its poverty should be more glorious than the first, because Christ, the Desire of all nations, should come to it. The Lord of hosts should fill it with glory. This teaches us that it is not the outward building—not the house, but the Presence that sanctifies the house, that constitutes its glory. "In this place will I give peace." It is His prerogative to bestow it.

# JUNE 5

*When ye shall have done all those things which are commanded you, say, We are unprofitable servants.*—Luke 17:10

Our Lord teaches us here that there is no merit in our obedience. Whatever our works may be, however unceasing and self-denying, they never make God our debtor. It is our duty and our privilege to serve Him. He has a full claim on all we are, as well as on what we have. The powers and faculties of mind and body, the influence and opportunities we enjoy, and the time we have at our disposal are all gifts that come directly from Him. With these we have to trade. "Occupy till I come." If at the last we can come to Him, bringing ten or five pounds as the result of our trading, we shall have to say, *"Thy* pound hath gained" this profit. Not unto us, O Lord, not unto us, but unto Thy name be the glory. The word "unprofitable," though it denotes in English the opposite of profit, is here used in a negative sense, and is equivalent to "We have not profited or benefited God at all by our services." We cannot, even by our most devoted service, lay God under any obligation to us. Those who serve God best receive far more than they can give.

# JUNE 6

*He will rest in his love.*—Zeph. 3:17

Or, "He will be silent in His love." "For," as the late Rev. James Vaughan says, "there is rest beyond language, whose very eloquence it is that it cannot choose but to be silent." The words should be considered in connection with the other portion of the verse; for it is like a jewel that shines all the brighter because of its setting. "The Lord thy God in the midst of thee is mighty." That declares to us a fact full of deep comfort and encouragement. "The Lord thy God." That shows His Covenant relationship—*"thy* God." Then we have the thought of His nearness: "In the midst of thee"; and the special attribute that belongs to Him: He "is mighty." We are now prepared to consider what He will do, how He will manifest Himself. "He will save, he will rejoice over thee with joy; he will rest in his love, he will joy over thee with singing." The satisfaction here implied is the Savior's own joy arising out of the salvation of His people. He has a joy of benevolence, and a joy of complacency. "Who for the joy that was set before him," the joy of saving lost sinners, "endured the cross, despising the shame."

# JUNE 7

*Men ought always to pray, and not to faint.*—Luke 18:1

All our Lord's parables were given with a definite end— a special object. Here in the context is a parable "to this end, that men ought always to pray, and not to faint." The words are intended, it would seem, not so much for those who do not pray, but for those who pray but do not *continue* in prayer. The Lord bids us "always to pray," which we may understand in the sense of keeping on, persevering in prayer. There is a special danger of yielding to the unbelieving suggestion that, after all, prayer has no power in it—that it is useless to persist in our supplications—that if we have offered up our petition it is enough. If the answer comes—well; but if not, it will not come because of our importunity. The parable and our Lord's teaching in connection with it are directly opposed to such an unbelieving view. Here we are taught plainly that it is God's will that we should ask, and ask again. It is no proof that God does not hear us because the answer is delayed; nor is the delay a sign that the petition is denied. We must "continue in prayer, and watch in the same with thanksgiving."

# JUNE 8

*The LORD made all that he did to prosper in his hand.*
   —Gen. 39:3

This is the privilege of that soul who walks before God and seeks His smile rather than his own selfish ends and personal advancement. We read, "The LORD was with Joseph," and it was also true that Joseph was with the Lord. This is to say, his desires and thoughts and will were with Him. This was true of Joseph in the prison as well as in the palace, in adversity as well as in prosperity. The above is recorded of him before his sore trial and false imprisonment. "The LORD made all that he did to prosper in his hand." "The LORD blessed the Egyptian's house for Joseph's sake." But what do we read of him when he is cast into prison? The same thing is again recorded. "But the LORD was with Joseph, and shewed him mercy, and gave him favour in the sight of the keeper of the prison. And the keeper of the prison committed to Joseph's hand all the prisoners that were in the prison; and whatsoever they did there, he was the doer of it" (vv. 21, 22). Here again we see God's blessing resting on Him. Let us learn from this that both temporal and spiritual prosperity have but one source.

# JUNE 9

*Never man spake like this man.*—John 7:46

Such was the witness of those men who were sent by the enemies of our Lord to take Him. There was something in His words, the power of His testimony, that completely disarmed them, and made them feel it was impossible to lay hands on Him. They saw what they supposed was only an ordinary man, but "in him dwelt all the fulness of the Godhead bodily." The words that He spake not only reached their ears, they penetrated down into their hearts. They searched out the secrets that were hidden therein. As they listened they felt like the woman of Samaria: Here is a man that hath "told me all things that ever I did: is not this the Christ?" "Never man spake like this man." Never man had such knowledge of the human heart; never man was so able to reach it. "They were astonished at his doctrine: for he taught them as one that had authority, and not as the scribes" (Mark 1:22). And again in another place we read, "They were astonished at his doctrine: for his word was with power" (Luke 4:32).

# JUNE 10

*The younger son ... took his journey into a far country, and
there wasted his substance with riotous living.*—Luke 15:13

The spirit of this younger son has been thus described.
He was "weary of restraint, panting for independence,
unable longer to abide the check of a father's eye." This
is the spirit of man in his estrangement from God. He
seeks to be his own master. The parable teaches us that
as the father yielded to his son's request, so God permits
us to make the trial of seeking our own pleasure in forgetfulness of Him. Along that road of self-will and self-
seeking, man passes from bad to worse, till at length, like
the prodigal, he comes to his last extremity. We have to
thank God there is always a famine in the land that is
far away from God. But even when the famine came,
the prodigal was not humbled sufficiently to allow of his
turning his steps homeward. He must needs better his
condition first. But self-efforts to better our condition
bring us into lower depths of misery and degradation. He
becomes a swineherd. It was then, in his hunger and
despair, that the crisis came.

# JUNE 11

*He arose, and came to his father. But when he was yet a
great way off, his father saw him, and had compassion, and
ran, and fell on his neck, and kissed him.*—Luke 15:20

Having come to himself, the prodigal no longer wastes
his time in vain regrets, but acts at once on the resolution
to which he had come. "He arose, and came to his
father." This is the story of every true conversion. Many
are convicted who are not converted. Paul tells us how
the Thessalonian converts "turned to God from idols."
There is not only to be a turning *from* the evil, but a
turning *to* God. So the prodigal came to his father. No
doubt he thought the journey home would be as long
as the journey into the far country. But it was not so. The
Father always meets the soul that sincerely seeks Him.
Even when we are a great way off, the Father sees us,
and knows all about us. The parable gives us a picture
of divine reconciliation. It is our blessed Lord's own
picture. We may rely, then, upon its being a true and
faithful representation of what actually takes place when
the soul in contrition and penitence comes to the feet of
Jesus. The whole parable sets forth the joy that there is
on God's side over every sinner that repents.

## JUNE 12

*Every thing that may abide the fire, ye shall make it go through the fire, and it shall be clean.*—Num. 31:23

Water and fire were the means used for ceremonial purification. There were things to be cleansed that could not stand the fire; these were purified by water. And there were other things, such as metals, that could not be purified by water; these were cleansed by fire. The spoils of the Midianites required purification, not only as being tainted with death, but as having been heathen property. But, of course, all this was typical. These laws were intended to impress Israel with the fact that the God of heaven was a holy God, and that they were called to be a holy people. "Whatever is to be brought over from the natural life of passion, into the sanctified life of grace, must be purged by the cleansing virtue of the Atonement (the 'water of separation,' see Num. 19). and by the baptism of the Holy Spirit. Nothing which has been contaminated with sin can be turned to Christian uses unless it is first sanctified, according to its nature. But, subject to this purifying, all that is not in itself sinful may be adapted to Christian ends and used by Christian people."

## JUNE 13

*Abide in me, and I in you.*—John 15:4

We ought to notice the order of this twofold abiding. The condition of having the Lord dwelling in us is, that we ourselves should be dwelling in Him. We must abide in Him if we would have Him abiding in us. The whole chapter sets forth the deep and mysterious truth of the soul's union with Christ. There is a union of life, and there is a union of will. Fellowship cannot be known unless the latter, as well as the former, is a reality in our experience.

Another point we must remember, which is declared in this chapter is this—Christ is not the root or the stem only; He is the whole vine. "I am the vine." So that what Christ is covers every branch and every leaf and every tendril of the whole plant. Just as in another place the name "Christ" is given to the whole body (see 1 Cor. 12:12). The believer is to abide in Christ as the branch abides in the vine. The function of the branch is to maintain connection with the stem, to receive the life-sap at one end, and to bear the fruit at the other. The branch cannot *produce* fruit—its duty is to *bear* it.

# JUNE 14

*As the sufferings of Christ abound in us, so our consolation
also aboundeth by Christ.*—2 Cor. 1:5

What were the sufferings to which the apostle here refers?
They were "the sufferings endured, whether by Himself or
by His Church with which He identified Himself." Christ
calls His people's sufferings His own. "Because of the
sympathy and mystical union between Him and us (Rom.
8:17; 1 Cor. 4:10; Heb. 2:17, 18), Christ's own sufferings
are revived in His people's (Ch. 4:10)." "They are borne for
His sake. They tend to His glory (Eph. 4:1; 1 Pet. 4:14, 16)."

But though the sufferings are many, the consolation
exceeds them. The apostle continually dwells, in his epistles, on the subject of comfort. He shows us how each
Person of the Trinity ministers to the consolation of the
people of God, and that a restful heart is as essential to
our work and progress as a strong and courageous heart.
In fact, comfort is the secret of strength and courage. Joy
and suffering are often in the apostle's mind as the paradox of the Christian life. "As sorrowful, yet always rejoicing."

# JUNE 15

*The secret things belong unto the Lord our God; but those
which are revealed belong unto us.*—Deut. 29:29

The "secret things" here were the things which God had
*not* revealed regarding Israel's future. These belonged to
the Lord. They were not to pry into them, as they were
prone to do, with eager curiosity. The Lord had given
them to know enough on which to occupy their thoughts
and exercise their faith. He had revealed sufficient for
their walk of obedience. The truth to be drawn from the
passage is, that the Bible is primarily a book for practical
guidance, not for the solution of speculative difficulties
or the gratification of a vain curiosity.

But many truths that were mysteries then, when these
words were written, are now revealed. They are no longer
hidden, but made known. We live in days of full Gospel
light. And this light is given us for action; for the work
of faith, and not for curious speculations. The secret of
getting more light lies in obedience to the measure of
light we already have. Let us "walk while we have the
light." That word "walk" points to practical obedience.

# JUNE 16

*See then that ye walk circumspectly, not as fools, but as wise, redeeming the time, because the days are evil.*
—Eph. 5:15, 16

"See then how ye walk with exactness," is Bishop Ellicott's translation. There is here a double idea—"See *how* ye walk," and *"that* ye walk circumspectly." Both the *manner* of the walk and the *act* of walking are included in the thought. It is of the first importance that we take heed to the manner in which we walk before men. "Walk in wisdom toward them that are without." Be not indifferent to the fact that you may be misunderstood. While we are not to walk so as to please men, let us not err on the other side and so walk that our good is evil spoken of. Let us walk accurately, correctly, in relation to unbelievers, so that we give no occasion of stumbling.

"Buying up for yourselves the seasonable time." "Special seasons for good occasionally present themselves, of which believers ought diligently to avail themselves." All this implies an attitude of trust, a spirit of prayer, and a habit of holy vigilance. It is only as that is true, that we can walk circumspectly.

# JUNE 17

*In every thing by prayer and supplication with thanksgiving let your requests be made known unto God.*—Phil. 4:6

The apostle warns them against anxiety. "Be careful for nothing." Be not anxious concerning anything—"but in everything by prayer." This is one of the means by which to guard against worry. Turn your trouble or anxiety into prayer. Let it be definite and specific. Let it be earnest and full of praise. The remembrance of past mercies will not only strengthen our faith and lead us to expect future blessings—it will help us to be more real and child-like in prayer. A special promise belongs to this precept, and follows it immediately: "And the peace of God, which passeth all understanding, shall keep your hearts and minds through Christ Jesus." It is in vain we pray to be kept, if we neglect to obey the Lord's direction. The burdens and cares that come upon us daily we must commit to the Lord daily. It is as we fulfill the condition that we shall find the truth of the promise. God will surely fulfill His own undertaking, but He expects us to be obedient to His will.

## JUNE 18

*Thou shalt put the mercy seat above upon the ark ... and there I will meet with thee.*—Exod. 25:21, 22

"There I will meet with thee." Let us consider the *place* that God had chosen—the place where He had appointed to meet with His people, in the person of the high priest. It was "from above the mercy seat." The mercy seat was the golden lid that covered the Ark. It was a cover —not a cover in the ordinary sense, but a propitiatory covering. The same word is translated in the New Testament "propitiation." "He is the propitiation for our sins" (the mercy seat); and again: "Whom God hath set forth to be a propitiation" (mercy seat) (1 John 2:2; Rom. 3:25). Again, it was "upon the ark of the testimony." The Ark or chest formed the basis of God's throne. It was on this the mercy seat rested. What did the Ark typify? As the golden lid pointed to Christ in His propitiatory sacrifice, so the Ark itself was a type of His complex nature —the fine wood pointing to His humanity, the pure gold to His deity. Taken together—the mercy seat and the Ark of the covenant—they are but types of the Person and work of the Lord Jesus Christ.

## JUNE 19

*Holiness, without which no man shall see the Lord.* —Heb. 12:14

Christ is made of God unto us not righteousness only, but also holiness, and without that holiness no man shall see the Lord. Holiness is not the same as righteousness. Righteousness is that which meets a just claim. Because of man's transgression there was a righteous claim that had to be met, which man himself was utterly unable to meet. Christ is made of God unto us righteousness, and as such perfectly satisfies every righteous claim that the law has upon us. But in addition to this, because God is not only a righteous Judge, but a gracious and loving Father, there were requirements that came from His heart as well as from His law. God's heart needed to be satisfied. Nothing but a perfect response to the claims of His infinitely pure and holy nature could satisfy His heart. It was this that Christ, as the perfect Man—God's ideal— actually accomplished, and so was made unto us, became on our behalf, "holiness" as well as "righteousness." Without that holiness no man shall see the Lord.

## JUNE 20

*Take this child away, and nurse it for me, and I will give thee thy wages.*—Exod. 2:9

In the most natural way possible, Moses was rescued by Pharaoh's daughter, restored to his mother to nurse, adopted by the princess as her son, and afterward educated by her in a way suitable to his position. Certain important advantages were thus secured to him. He had safe protection, a liberal education, and experience of court life in Egypt. All this was needful in order to fit him for the great responsibilities of his future office and calling. We see how Pharaoh's plans were foiled by his own daughter. His edict was made the means of introducing to his own court the future deliverer of the race he meant to destroy. Thus God takes the wicked in their own net (Ps. 9:15, 16).

"By faith Moses, when he was born, was hid three months of his parents, because they saw he was a proper child; and they were not afraid of the king's commandment" (Heb. 11:23). His parents did not allow the fear of man to influence their conduct. They had faith in God that He would give success to their endeavor.

## JUNE 21

*Christ also suffered for us, leaving us an example, that ye should follow his steps.*—1 Pet. 2:21

Archbishop Leighton observes on this passage, "The Captain, or Leader, of our salvation, as the Apostle speaks, was consecrated by suffering (Heb. 2:10); that was the way by which He entered into the holy place, where He is now our everlasting High Priest, making intercession for us. If He be our Leader to salvation, must not we follow Him in the way He leads, whatsoever it be? If it be (as we see it is) by way of sufferings, we must either follow on in that way, or fall short of salvation; for there is no other leader, nor any other way than that which He opened." "Leaving us an example," or, as it may be translated, "a writing copy," set by masters for their pupils. He left His footsteps as a copy for us to follow. We have to follow Him not in His outward conduct merely, but in His inner life of self-renunciation and trust in His Father's word. To try to follow His steps in outward action, without being like Him in the inner principles that prompted Him in all His ways, is to endeavor to bring forth fruit without a root.

## JUNE 22

*Ye are dead, and your life is hid with Christ in God.*—Col. 3:3

More literally it is, *"For ye died."* The words do not describe a *condition of deadness,* as many have assumed, but they point to the fact that death, as a crisis, has been passed through. And if we recognize the principle that all the great *facts* of redemption find their accomplishment first of all in Christ, rather than in our individual experience, then we see that the death referred to took place on the cross. "For ye died" with Christ when He died. You were identified with Him in His death. This is the meaning of your baptism. "Know ye not, that so many of us as were baptized into Jesus Christ were baptized into his death?" "Into *his* death," remember, not into *your* death. The fact with which faith is concerned is not something which finds its center in yourself, but in Christ. "For ye died." When? When you were baptized? No. When you experienced that wonderful blessing? No. But when *Christ* died, and you, in the eye of God, died with Him. This is the foundation of all experimental knowledge. We must begin with the judicial fact, or we shall have no solid basis to rest upon.

## JUNE 23

*I will pray the Father, and he shall give you another Comforter . . . even the Spirit of truth.*—John 14:16, 17

We can understand how truly the disciples felt that Christ was their Comforter. To lose Him would seem to them to be bereft of the one great source of consolation. As far as His visible presence was concerned, He was about to withdraw Himself from them. To those who clung to the outward Man this was a sore trial. But He tells them that He was about to send them another Comforter. Not that He Himself in His real spiritual Presence would no longer be with them. For He says expressly, "I will not leave you comfortless [orphans]; I will come to you." And again He declares concerning His spiritual Presence, "And, lo, *I am* with you alway" (Matt. 28:20). It would still be true that in Him they should have peace (John 16:33). The privileges of the Gospel dispensation would not grow less as His redemption advanced; nay, they would increase. They should have Him still with them— though not in the same way—and they should have *another* Comforter in addition.

## JUNE 24

*The ark of the covenant of the* LORD *went before them . . . to search out a resting place for them.*—Num. 10:33

After we are brought to know the blessings of deliverance, we are then ready to learn the secret of guidance. How wonderful is the sight here presented to us! Instead of Israel seeking to find a resting place for God, it is God who would find a resting place for them. Shelter and guidance were here provided for His redeemed people. "The cloud of the LORD was upon them by day, when they went out of the camp." They were thus protected from the scorching rays of the midday sun. And "the ark of the covenant of the LORD went before them," in order to show them the path of His will. They were not left to choose their own way, or to use their own wisdom in discovering God's way. The symbol of the divine Presence preceded them. They had but to follow. And so it is with all God's children today. He who died to redeem, now lives to lead and direct. He seeks for us continually not merely places of safety, but of "rest." He is concerned about His people, and delights in their comfort and joy.

## JUNE 25

*When he shall appear, we shall be like him, for we shall see him as he is.*—1 John 3:2

Two thoughts are here suggested: the likeness and the vision. The likeness is the effect of the vision. As to the likeness, there is the image we have to bear in the present, and there is the image we shall bear in the future: "Beholding as in a glass the glory of the Lord, [we] are changed [being changed] into the same image from glory to glory" (2 Cor. 3:18). This is a spiritual transfiguration that is going on now progressively. The image of the Lord Jesus is to be seen in the believer now. This is God's purpose, that we might "be conformed to the image of his Son" (Rom. 8:29). But this image, as it is reflected in us, is, after all, but an imperfect likeness. "When he shall appear"—when He shall be manifested, that is, at His coming—"we shall be like him." Not in spirit only, but in body also. The likeness will then be perfect and complete. That is in the future. But both the likeness we have to bear in the present, and that which we will bear in the future, depend upon the vision we have of Christ. Now we see "through a glass darkly; then face to face."

# JUNE 26

*Oh that thou wouldest bless me indeed . . . and that thou wouldest keep me from evil! . . . And God granted him that which he requested.*—1 Chron. 4:10

It is a great thing to be convinced that all blessing comes from God alone; that "every good gift and every perfect gift is from above, and cometh down from the Father of lights, with whom is no variableness, neither shadow of turning" (James 1:17). How prone we are to think that *some* blessings are to be sought in other directions! Jabez had learned this lesson. Then again, we have to learn how inseparable all real happiness is from a condition of deliverance from the power and service of sin. "Keep me from evil," was the earnest desire of this man of prayer. Our Lord asked in behalf of His disciples, "I pray not that thou shouldest take them out of the world, but that thou shouldest keep them from evil" (John 17:15). The blessings connected with God's keeping power are not negative merely. Looked at all around, we find they included all positive privileges.

# JUNE 27

*Who shall be able to stand?*—Rev. 6:17

These words refer to that awful day when those who have rejected Christ shall hide "themselves in the dens and in the rocks of the mountains," and shall say "to the mountains and rocks, Fall on us, and hide us from the face of him that sitteth on the throne, and from the wrath of the Lamb: for the great day of his wrath is come." And "who," it is asked, "shall be able to stand?"

That question is one of major importance now. For if we would stand in safety and acceptance hereafter, before the all-seeing One, in His unclouded glory, we must know what it is to "stand" in peace and safety now.

"Being justified by faith, we have peace with God through our Lord Jesus Christ; by whom also we have access by faith *into this grace wherein we stand*" (Rom. 5:1, 2). We stand in the grace of a present acceptance. We stand "in Christ," not having our own righteousness, which is of the law, but that which is through the faith of Christ, the righteousness which is of God through faith (Phil. 3:9). It is in that divine righteousness we stand, acquitted of every charge and justified from all things.

## JUNE 28

*I know that my redeemer liveth.*—Job 19:25

This was testimony to a personal interest in God's salvation. He says, "*my* redeemer." Many have a faith in Christ as the Redeemer of men generally. But religion has but little power in our lives until it becomes an individual matter. It is when we can thus appropriate God's unspeakable Gift, and say from our hearts, "Thou art *my* Savior, '*my* Lord and *my* God,'" that the comfort and strength of His redemption are realized. It is then, but not before, that we can take our stand as witnesses to His saving grace.

Job speaks, too, without doubt or hesitation. He does not say, "I hope," but, "I *know* that my redeemer liveth." There are some who regard such expressions as too presumptuous for sinful men to adopt. Well, it depends upon what our confidence is based. Is it confidence in what we have done, or are, upon what we have attained? Then, most certainly, such language is utterly unsuitable, for creatures such as we are, to use. But if it is confidence *in the Lord*—in His word of assurance, in His promise, in what He has done, and undertakes still to do—then it is impossible to trust too confidently.

## JUNE 29

*His commandments are not grievous.*—1 John 5:3

How is it that many think they are? Well, you say, because they have never been "born again." To those who are unrenewed, all God's requirements are irksome. True, but how is it that to many who have been converted to God, who have been born of the Spirit, His commandments are, very often, hard and irksome? The answer is to be sought, not in the fact of a new nature alone being needed, but also in a right disposition of heart, in addition to the new nature, being essential to all happy and harmonious walking with God along the line of His will.

Here, then, is a useful test in ascertaining our true spiritual condition. How do I regard God's commandments? Do I take the comfort of His promises, while at the same time I turn aside from His commands?

To be in a right condition of soul is to be finding as much liberty and encouragement in what God requires of us as in what He bestows on us.

## JUNE 30

*As many as I love, I rebuke and chasten.*—Rev. 3:19

We are told that the word translated "chasten" means in classical Greek to *instruct,* but in the New Testament to instruct by *chastisement* (Heb. 12:5, 6). Chastening describes God's dealings with His erring children; punishment seems to express His dealings with rebellious sinners. Here we have language that has reference to a true Church, but a Church in a backsliding condition. The Lord was no longer enshrined within. He was standing without, seeking an entrance. Very solemn, searching, and strong are the words of warning used, and yet how full of tenderness and love they are! This church of the Laodiceans has a special voice to us who live in these the closing days of the dispensation. It presents to us, as we believe, the characteristic features of the evils that are peculiar to these last days. To every child of God whose heart has grown cold and worldly the Lord of Glory appeals in words of solemn, faithful, but tenderest love. He stands at the door of the heart into which the world has come and crowded out the holy thoughts and affections that once occupied it. And as He stands He says, "I love," "I rebuke," "I chasten."

## JULY 1

*The fruit of the Spirit is ... goodness.*—Gal. 5:22

This quality belongs to the second division of the three triplets into which the fruit of the Spirit may be divided. The first set of three comprises "Christian habits of mind," as Bishop Lightfoot says, "Love, joy, and peace," or the inner spiritual *condition* of the man. Then comes the second set of three, "Longsuffering, gentleness, goodness." These, as the same author remarks, are "special qualities affecting a man's intercourse with his neighbor," or the outer *conduct.* The last three "exhibit the principles which guide a Christian's conduct," or the *character* of the man. But let us remember they are all the product in us of the Holy Ghost. "Goodness" has been defined as "the quality of him who is ruled by, and aims at, the good. Moral worth, and sterling goodness, apart from attractiveness." And although each quality may be considered separately, let us not forget they cannot exist alone; they together form one bunch, so to speak—they are the one *"fruit* of the Spirit."

# JULY 2

*This is the ordinance of the passover: There shall no stranger eat thereof.*—Exod. 12:43

The Passover was a feast for the Lord's people. Only those who had been brought into covenant with God by circumcision were allowed to partake of this feast. Circumcision has its antitype in the cross. As the ordinance of circumcision separated the Israel of God from all the nations of the earth, so the cross of the Lord Jesus Christ separates the Church from the world. Those who partook of this feast, moreover, were sheltered by the blood; so it is only those who are covered by the atoning sacrifice of Christ that have a right to partake of this ordinance. "No stranger shall eat thereof." The truth is, there can be no real spiritual reception until the soul is born again. The Lord's Supper, of which the Passover was the type, is a memorial and a thanksgiving, but it is also a feast. Do we know what it is to feed on Christ in our hearts by faith, as well as to believe that He died for our sins on Calvary's cross?

# JULY 3

*If children, then heirs; heirs of God, and joint-heirs with Christ.*
—Rom. 8:17

*Sonship* being proved, the Apostle proceeds to show that *Heirship* follows as a natural consequence. The "Heir of all things" is the Lord Jesus Christ. He is the "sole Proprietor of the vast creation of God, and He has admitted us to claim the whole as ours, by virtue of that deed of joint heirship which the Lord hath ratified with His chosen people. . . . All that He has He shares with His people." It is His delight to bring us into participation of all the wealth that belongs to Him. "As having nothing, and yet possessing all things" (2 Cor. 6:10). "All things are yours" (1 Cor. 3:21). The first thing to know is our sonship. Am I a child? Have I been born into the family of God? The apostle tells us in this chapter that it is the Holy Ghost who bears "witness with our spirit, that we are the children of God." Sonship is not an attainment. It is a privilege that belongs to the youngest believer as much as to the most advanced and mature of saints.

"Because ye are sons, God hath sent forth the Spirit of his Son into your hearts . . ." (Gal. 4:6).

# JULY 4

*Leaning on Jesus' bosom.*—John 13:23

The place of closest fellowship, of sweetest rest, of perfect peace. It is of the disciple whom Jesus loved that this is recorded. That was the one to whom the Lord would most likely reveal His secret, so the other disciples thought. There are many things the Lord has to tell us that we are not able to hear—not ready to receive, because we do not walk in sufficiently close communion with Him. We must be very near Him to hear His whispers. We may understand His truths and grasp firmly His doctrine, and yet we may not see His Person. "I will manifest *Myself* to him" is the promise that belongs to the obedient disciple. That is, I will make Myself to him "a living bright reality" —One on whom you may lean, to whom you may tell all the secrets of your heart, and on whose love you may confidently and continually rely. It is the *reality* of Christ's presence of which so many of God's children need to be convinced. Let *Him* be recognized as with us in the scenes of daily life, and not only will our faith be strengthened, our love will be brought into exercise. It is not only more faith but more love we need—love to Christ as a personal and ever-present Savior and Friend.

# JULY 5

*We have known and believed the love that God hath to us.* —1 John 4:16

John tells us in the 20th chapter of his gospel, the 31st verse, that the purpose of that Gospel was "that ye might *believe.*" And in his epistle (1 John 5:13) he says, "These things have I written . . . that ye may *know.*" Believe what? "That Jesus is the Christ, the Son of God; and that believing, ye *might have life* through his name." Know what? "That ye *have eternal life.*" So it is possible to believe, and yet not to know. There may be faith—real saving faith—and yet there may be no assurance. The first gives life; the second gives comfort and power. "We have known," says the apostle, as well as "believed the love that God hath to us." That love not only gladdens our hearts, it transforms our characters. It is not only a manifestation that has drawn us into His presence, it is an indwelling power that makes us like Him. This was our Lord's prayer—"That the love wherewith thou hast loved me may be in them, and I in them" (John 17:26).

# JULY 6

*Let your speech be alway with grace.*—Col. 4:6

"*In* grace as its element, investiture" (Eph. 4:29; Col. 3:16). Atmosphere is an important factor, whether we think of the natural or the spiritual world. Grace is the true sphere of the child of God. But grace has two important aspects. We may regard it as the ground on which God has dealt with us in Jesus Christ. "By grace are ye saved" (Eph. 2:8). It is that which regards our demerit. And then grace is that which meets our need, after He has removed our guilt. "My grace is sufficient for thee" (2 Cor. 12:9). We think of our guilt, and we see how God has dealt with us in grace. And we think of our emptiness, and we see how God meets it with His grace. In the first it is the opposite of merit; in the second it is the complement of our need.

Our very speech ought to show that we are the subjects of divine grace. We may minister grace to those who hear our words. Let the Lord of grace fill the heart, and control every thought and desire, and then from the lips will flow words of quickening grace.

# JULY 7

*Then was Jesus led up of the Spirit into the wilderness to be tempted of the devil.*—Matt. 4:1

"Then,"—that is, immediately after His baptism by the Holy Ghost, Christ was anointed for service. This spiritual equipment was intended for work and for conflict, for trial and temptation. So it must be with us. Times of special blessing, of peculiar spiritual enlightenment or enduement, are not intended for lives of inactivity or of ordinary duties. They are the preparation for special service, for fierce conflict, for greater usefulness. It is the Holy Spirit who must lead. Even our Lord did not place Himself in these circumstances of trial. He was led of the Spirit. So we must be on our guard lest our trials or temptations are self-imposed. It is possible to run before the Spirit. We may find ourselves in scenes of alluring temptations, into which the Holy Ghost has never brought us. We have come there ourselves. This is to tempt God. But where the Spirit leads us, there will the Spirit clothe us. The whole armor of God is always available as long as we are led of the Spirit. And it is impenetrable.

# JULY 8

*If we confess our sins, he is faithful and just to forgive us our sins, and to cleanse us from all unrighteousness.* —1 John 1:9

This confession is not a mere acknowledgment of sins in general, but points to specific and definite acts. Now if we, being conscious of sins, confess them to God, what is it that we may expect? "He is *faithful* and *just* to forgive." How many a sin-burdened soul has stumbled at these words! How can God be *just* to forgive? Is not His justice on the side of our condemnation? If the words had been "He is gracious and merciful to forgive," there would have been no difficulty in understanding them. And yet, when rightly understood, the words as they stand in the Scripture are full of far deeper comfort and encouragement than if God's attributes of grace and mercy had occupied their place. For we have here a Father's revelation of the fact that our pardon rests on infinite justice in carrying out the terms of the covenant which He made with His Son, when that Son undertook to meet all the claims of Gods' righteous law on our behalf. The Son having completed His side of the eternal covenant, the Father binds Himself to fulfill His.


# JULY 9

*I have caused thine iniquity to pass from thee, and I will clothe thee with change of raiment.*—Zech. 3:4

It is the Angel of the Covenant that utters these words. *I* have done this. None but Jehovah could "cause iniquity to pass away." The change of raiment could not take place until the iniquity was done away. This denoted the putting on of priestly vestments. These were new and clean, instead of those that were old and soiled. The spiritual significance of all this would appear to be, first, divine pardon and cleansing, and then the restoration of the pardoned one to the privileges of priestly service. They could no longer render to God acceptable service. How true is this of the child of God who, through sin in some form or other, is no longer serving in the power of the Spirit! Such a one needs something more than pardon. He needs to hear the Lord's voice saying unto him, "I have caused thine iniquity to pass from thee, and I will clothe thee with change of raiment."

## JULY 10

*The disciple is not above his master.*—Matt. 10:24

A disciple is a learner. A learner, not only of the Lord's truth, but of the Lord's humility. He has to follow his Master both in doctrine and in suffering. He must always be at his Master's feet. He must never be above his Master. And so the true disciple finds that in following he has perpetually to descend. For his Master is the very embodiment of humility. He "made himself of no reputation"—emptied Himself. And the disciple must not seek for himself anything above that which his Master sought for Himself. "It is enough for the disciple that he be as his master, and the servant as his lord." The Master was among us as one that served. Though Lord of all, He took the place of a servant. It was as such He glorified His Father. It is as such that we shall glorify our Lord. O for this spirit of self-abnegation—this mind which was in Christ Jesus! There is no real following until we know what it is to ignore self. "If any man will come after me, let him deny himself, and take up his cross, and follow me" (Matt. 16:24). This denial of self is not the end, but the condition of following the Master.

## JULY 11

*I am with thee to save thee and to deliver thee, saith the* LORD.
—Jer. 15:20

"Jehovah had promised Jeremiah protection from his enemies. His infirmity suggests that God had failed to do so." God's reply to Jeremiah is, "If thou return, then will I bring thee again, and thou shalt stand before me: and if thou take forth the precious from the vile, thou shalt be as my mouth: let them return unto thee; but return not thou unto them." Then comes the promise so full of gracious encouragement, of which the text above is a part. And what the Lord declares He will do for the prophet, every true witness for Christ may take as a divine assurance for himself: "I am with thee to save thee and to deliver thee." A saved soul needs a daily salvation and a perpetual deliverance. He needs not only to be continually delivered out of the hand of the wicked, he needs to be saved from evil thoughts and desires, he needs to be kept in a state of deliverance from self-seeking and self-confidence. This salvation is found in the Lord's perpetual manifestation of Himself. "I am with thee."

# JULY 12

*My presence shall go with thee, and I will give thee rest.*
—Exod. 33:14

Owing to Israel's apostasy in returning to the idolatry of
Egypt during the absence of Moses in the Mount, the
Lord had declared He could no longer continue to take
up His abode in their midst. "And Moses took the tent"
(not the tabernacle, for that had not yet been reared—
probably his own tent), "and pitched it without the camp,
afar off from the camp, and called it the Tabernacle of
the congregation." This was Israel's relation to the divine Presence. And God now threatened to withdraw
that Presence from them altogether. He consented to drive
out their enemies before them, and to give them the
land; but He said, "I will not go up *in the midst* of thee."
Moses felt that if His Presence were withheld, no matter
what other blessings might be granted, they would all be
as nothing in comparison with that one essential and all-
inclusive privilege. So Moses said, "If thy presence go
not with me, carry us not up hence." Jehovah was gracious to His people, and granted to Moses, in spite of
their rebellion, his request. "My presence shall go with
thee, and I will give thee rest."

# JULY 13

*I am my beloved's, and his desire is toward me.*—Song of
Sol. 7:10

This is the language of the Bride, or the Church, to her
Lord. She rejoices in the thought not only that Christ is
hers, but also that she is Christ's. The first thing needful
is that we should receive Him and know that He is ours.
This is salvation. The next thing is that we should give
ourselves to Him and know that we are His. Here is
the secret of service. "Whose I am" precedes "and whom
I serve." Many are trying to give their hearts to Christ
before they have received Christ into their hearts. The
gift of God is to lost and guilty sinners—not to those
who have improved their condition, or have consecrated
themselves to Him. But when we can say, "He is mine,"
then let us go on to learn what it is to say, "and I am
his (compare Song of Sol. 2:16 with 7:10). Then, again,
we see the Bridegroom's heart toward the Bride. The desire of Christ toward the Church is that of Savior and Husband. "He loved the church, and gave himself for it."

# JULY 14

*Out of the abundance of the heart the mouth speaketh.*
—Matt. 12:34

What is the heart? It is that central region of our being where three things are focused: the thoughts, the desires, and the will. Every one is constantly thinking and desiring and willing; and the nature and current of his thoughts, the character and aim of his desires, as well as the attitude and direction of his will, determine the state of the heart. The heart is neither the evil nature nor the new nature. The man who by God's grace is regenerated has received a new nature, and cannot become unregenerate though he may degenerate. But his heart may change from day to day. Today the Lord's beatitude may belong to him—"Blessed are the pure in heart"; tomorrow he may relapse into sin and lose that blessing. Now it is our privilege and our duty to be cleansed in thought and in desire, to be brought into a condition of loyalty in will and purpose, and to be kept in this state of inward conformity to Christ, moment by moment. "Faithful is he who hath called us, who also will do it." And the heart which the Lord cleanses He also fills.

# JULY 15

*Thy will be done in earth, as it is in heaven.*—Matt. 6:10

These words direct our thoughts to the obedience of angels. They are set before us as our pattern. The obedience of angels is in humility and perfect submission. The vision that the prophet Isaiah had of the divine glory revealed the seraphim in the beauty of their reverential submission to the divine will. "Each one had six wings; with twain he covered his face, and with twain he covered his feet, and with twain he did fly" (Isa. 6:2). We observe that, while two wings were used for action, four were needed as a covering. Without a deep sense of unworthiness we cannot fulfill the Lord's commands. Perhaps, in these days, it may be especially needful to remind ourselves that a reverential attitude of soul can alone become those who stand in the presence of the infinitely Holy One, the Lord of Hosts—our faces must be covered; and that, when we think of the imperfection of even our best service, our feet need to be covered. God's will is done in heaven reverentially, humbly, and promptly.

# JULY 16

*Ye shall be unto me a kingdom of priests, and an holy nation.*
—Exod. 19:6

Israel was at once a royal and a priestly race—they were both priests and kings. "There is no doubt," says Archbishop Leighton, "that this kingly priesthood is the common dignity of all believers: this honour have all the saints. They are kings, have victory and dominion given them over powers of darkness and the lusts of their own hearts, that held them captive and domineered over them before. . . . Now this is the benefit of receiving the kingdom of Christ into a man's heart, that it makes him a king himself. All the subjects of Christ are kings, not only in regard of that pure crown of glory they hope for, and shall certainly attain, but, in the present, they have a kingdom which is the pledge of that other, overcoming the world, and Satan, and themselves, by the power of faith. And so they 'are brought near unto God, and have access to the throne of His grace' (Heb. 10:21, 22). They resemble, in their spiritual state, the legal priesthood very clearly—(1) in their consecration; (2) in their service; and (3) in their laws of living."

# JULY 17

*Thou art a gracious God, and merciful, slow to anger, and of great kindness, and repentest thee of the evil.*—Jonah 4:2

The lesson taught in the parable of the Unforgiving Debtor was the lesson that Jonah needed at this time. Is it not the lesson we often need to learn in our dealings with others? We see here in the passage what was God's feeling on the repentance of Nineveh toward Him. He was ready to forgive. Then we see Jonah's feeling on the repentance of God toward Nineveh. He is hot with anger, and exceedingly displeased. Jonah was angry because of the judgments being withheld on account of Nineveh's repentance; it made him seem a false prophet. He thought of his own reputation rather than of God's glory and the welfare of precious souls. Jonah tries to excuse himself in fleeing into Tarshish, by saying that it was because he knew God would change His mind and not fulfill the judgments He commanded Jonah to proclaim. There are many lessons to be learned from Jonah. We need not only to obey the word of the Lord, but to be filled with the Spirit of Christ, and to work in sympathy with Him.

## JULY 18

*He calleth his own sheep by name, and leadeth them out.*
*—John 10:3*

These words suggest three precious thoughts. First, there
is divine *possession*. We who believe in Him belong to
the Good Shepherd. We are "his own sheep." He has set
His mark upon us. He distinguishes His own in a way
that they can never be confounded in His sight with those
who are of the world, Then, second, there is divine
*knowledge*. He says, "I know my sheep" (v. 14). He has
intimate acquaintance with them, so that He can call
each sheep by name. And then, third, there is divine
*guidance*. He "leadeth them out." He goes before them.
Each day He leads them into fresh pastures, into new
paths of service, into untrodden fields of patient following. If the Shepherd knows His sheep, it is that the sheep
may know their Shepherd. "I know my sheep, and am
known of mine." This mutual knowledge implies sympathy, love, community of nature (1 John 4:7; Gal. 4:9;
1 Cor. 8:3; John 17:3, 25). Christ first took our nature,
that we might afterward receive His. He who has laid
down His life for us, now gives His life to us.

## JULY 19

*He that is mighty hath done to me great things; and holy is*
*his name.—Luke 1:49*

What Mary said in a special sense, every heaven-born soul
can also say—"great things" has God done to me, "and
holy is His name." Every renewed heart, every enlightened
mind, every quickened soul, is a miracle of grace. "We
are his workmanship, created in Christ Jesus unto good
works" (Eph. 2:10). Nothing short of almighty power
could accomplish the change that takes place when a
soul passes from death to life. But holiness as well as
omnipotence stamps His work in every case of conversion. It is not only a passage from bondage to freedom,
from misery to joy, but also from sin to holiness, from
the service of Satan to God. "Holy is his name." We not
only rejoice that the tyranny and sorrow are over, we rejoice that the life of obedient and holy service has begun.
To Him we give all the glory. It is He who has wrought
the change. It is He by whose power the work has been
done; and by that same power are we kept faithful and
true. He who is Almighty to save is also Almighty to keep.

## JULY 20

*They are not of the world, even as I am not of the world.*
*—John 17:16*

This does not mean that our Lord did not care for the world. Our Lord did not pray that His disciples should be taken out of the world. But while they were in the world, they were not to be of the world. They were to be like their Master. "Even as I am not of the world." This did not mean a spirit of austerity, that is absorbed in its own selfish interest. Whoever appeared among the sons of men so full of tender sympathy, and so ready to welcome sinners, as the infinitely holy Lord Jesus Christ? No man ever came so close to the suffering and the needy as He who was altogether separate from sinners. The secret of being like the Master in this respect is not to be attained by rules and outward prescriptions. To have that mind in us which was also in Him, we must sanctify Christ as Lord in our hearts. There must be not only a oneness of life; but an identity of mind and will. How wonderfully the Lord Himself expresses it in the closing words of this marvellous prayer—"That the love wherewith thou hast loved me may be *in* them," not merely manifested toward them, "and I in them"!

## JULY 21

*What profit is there of circumcision?—Rom. 3:1*

It was generally granted that the elect people must have an advantage over the Gentiles. But from what the apostle had said it might be inferred that every advantage of the Jew was denied. It might be asked, "Will the people whom God has *elected,* and marked with the *seal* of this election, be treated exactly like the rest of the world?" As Professor Godet observes, "This objection is of the same nature as that which would be made in our day by a nominal Christian, if, when put face to face with God's sentence, he were to ask what advantage there accrues to him from his creed and baptism, if they are not to save him from condemnation." The apostle corrects the possible inference that the Jew, as such, had nothing special to thank God for. "The gift of Scripture brings the *responsibility* of the Jew into the fullest light." Let this thought fill us with a sense of our responsibilities—as we recognize the surpassing privileges which the Gospel has conferred upon us.

## JULY 22

*In that he died, he died unto sin once: but in that he liveth, he liveth unto God.*—Rom. 6:10

We give the Bishop of Durham's exposition of these words: "For as to His dying, it was as to our sin He died; it was to deal with our sin's claim; and He has dealt with it indeed, so that His death is 'once,' once for ever; but as to His living, it is as to God He lives; it is in relation to His Father's acceptance, it is as welcomed to His Father's throne for us, as the Slain One Risen. Even so must you too reckon yourselves, with the sure 'calculation' that His work for you. His life for you, is infinitely valid, to be dead indeed to your sin, dead in His atoning death, dead to the guilt exhausted by that death, but living to your God, in Christ Jesus; welcomed by your eternal Father, in your union with His Son, and in that union filled with a new and blessed life from your Head, to be spent in the Father's smile, on the Father's service."

It is into that reckoning we who believe are to enter. It is not a question of feeling or experience but of faith.

## JULY 23

*Then cometh the end.*—1 Cor. 15:24

"Then"—that is, after that—next in succession of "orders" or "ranks" "cometh the end." What is this end? Professor Godet says, "Used without qualification, as it is here, *the end* must designate the end absolutely speaking—'the end of all things, as Peter puts it (1 Pet. 4:7), the goal of the entire economy of education, redemption, and sanctification, the time when God's thought shall be at length fully realized in regard to man, come to his perfect stature in Christ." Chrysostom explains: the end of the *present age.* "Which is true only if we include within the present age the whole interval between the Advent and the end."

But what is it that shall mark this solemn epoch which the apostle calls "the end"? He explains in the following words: "When He shall have delivered up the kingdom to God, even the Father." The interval between the Lord's Advent and the end will be filled up by an epoch of judgment. Christ will during that time put down all powers. All things shall be brought into subjection unto Him. "For he must reign until he hath put all enemies under his feet."

# JULY 24

*Patient in tribulation.*—Rom. 12:12

The words that immediately precede our text are "rejoicing in hope." What are the links in the chain that unite "the rejoicing in hope" with this endurance in trial? They are given us in the fifth chapter of this epistle (vv. 2, 3, 4); we "rejoice in hope of the glory of God. And not only so, but we glory in tribulations also: knowing that tribulation worketh patience; and patience, experience; and experience, hope." Then if it is asked, How are we to maintain this joyful spring of hope, and this firmness of endurance in trial? the answer is found in the words that follow: "Continuing instant in prayer."

Perhaps there is no besetment to which we are more prone than that of impatience. Then how often, when we have endured in the great trial, we have broken down miserably under the small vexations and worries of ordinary life! And yet we have in Christ sufficient provision to overcome continually. "Strengthened with *all* might, according to his glorious power, unto *all* patience and longsuffering with joyfulness" (Col. 1:11).

# JULY 25

*We know that we have passed from death unto life.*—1 John 3:14

Salvation implies a transition from one sphere into another. "We have passed from death unto life." We have changed our state. We have come out of the old world into the new. Saving faith implies such a transition. Wherever it is spoken of in the Scriptures in reference to Christ as the object, it means to *believe in Him.* Before this step was taken we were in a state of darkness and death. But now we are in Him who is the life. This is true of all who have really trusted Him. And yet there are many who have life who have not the assurance of it. "We *know,*" says the apostle, "that we have passed from death unto life." "We know by the essential nature of our faith, by our own inward experience." And we know this "because we love the brethren." "The fact that we are conscious of a love for Christians as Christians is a proof to us that we have entered upon a new life; that we now first truly live. The passage has been made; the first new sphere of being has been gained. Life is not future, but present" *(Bishop Westcott).*

# JULY 26

*By faith Abraham, when he was called to go out into a place which he should after receive for an inheritance obeyed.*
—Heb. 11:8

With the call of Abraham commences a new period in the history of revelation. Abraham is the father of the faithful. He is a pattern of all believers. Abraham's faith was the substance of future things—things hoped for, and a conviction of things not seen. He not only left his home and kindred and went forth into a new land—he did all this in obedience to the call of God. "He went out, not knowing whither he went." He went forth relying on his God, "being fully persuaded that, what he had promised, he was able also to perform." "If you would believe," says Luther, "you must crucify the question, How?" God leads His people out today in precisely the same way. He gives them His word of promise. On that alone they have to lean. Difficulties and obstacles there are sure to be. But these must not hinder or discourage us. We must look *through* the things that are seen, and fix our eyes on Him who is invisible. It is in the trial of our faith that it grows. "He is able," is the great sheet anchor of our faith.

# JULY 27

*Christ, who is the image of God.*—2 Cor. 4:4

Christ is the substantial, true, living image of God's Being (Heb. 1:3). So that he that sees the Son sees the Father.

Adam was made "in the image of God" (Gen. 1:27). The second man, Christ, perfectly reflected "the invisible God." "Image" always supposes a prototype, from which it is drawn: the exact counterpart, as the reflection of the sun in the water, or as the impression on the wax corresponds to the seal. When Philip said, "Lord, shew us the Father, and it sufficeth us. Jesus saith unto him, Have I been so long time with you, and yet hast thou not known me, Philip? he that hath seen me hath seen the Father; and how sayest thou then, Shew us the Father?" (John 14:8, 9). But after all, it is a spiritual vision that is meant here. So many who saw Him with the outward eye, beheld no beauty that they should desire Him! (Isa. 53:2). "The god of this world hath blinded the minds of them which believe not, lest the light of the glorious gospel of Christ, who is the image of God, should shine unto them."

## JULY 28

*Walk in love.*—Eph. 5:2

Love is the power that has drawn us as sinners to God, that has melted the hardness of our hearts, and that now constrains us to live to Him. Love is the sphere of the Christian's activity. "God is love; and he that dwelleth in love dwelleth in God, and God in him" (1 John 4:16). We are called to be followers, imitators of God. Therefore we have to "walk in love." "God for Christ's sake hath forgiven you." If we imitate God in this respect we shall forgive one another. The apostle makes no distinction between our being the objects of God's love and our being the objects of the love of Christ. It is one and the same love. This love we have not only to contemplate and rejoice in, we have to "walk" in it. That is, we have to show it practically; we have to exemplify it. Walking is the phrase which the apostle uses to bring out the practical side of Christianity. As with our bodies so with our souls, we need exercise, in order to the full development of the life. We cannot remain in health unless we are carrying out into practice that which we have received as the cardinal truths of our faith.

## JULY 29

*Oh that thou wouldest rend the heavens, that thou wouldest come down.*—Isa. 64:1

"He, who had descended on Sinai, and taken up His abode in Israel, concealed the symbols of His Presence, the cherubim, behind a veil. That veil was once a year drawn aside to allow of atonement being made for the people's sins. But now God had retired from Israel, and hidden away His face behind a cloud of wrathful indignation. Could *that* veil ever be withdrawn? The prophet, in the Church's name, prays that it may be" *(Dr. Kay, Speakers' Comm.).* Nothing can compensate for the absence of the divine Presence. No matter what earthly blessings may be enjoyed or what advantages may be possessed, if the Lord is not present to reveal Himself, everything is vain, and nothing can prosper. The words express the intense longing of the prophet after the manifested Presence of Jehovah. May the same earnest thirsting after God be the constant characteristic of our lives! "As the hart panteth after the water brooks, so panteth my soul after thee, O God. My soul thirsteth for . . . the living God" (Ps. 42:1, 2).

# JULY 30

*Seek those things which are above, where Christ sitteth on the right hand of God.*—Col. 3:1

The exhortation is based on the fact that, as believers, we are risen with Christ. To be risen with Christ means that we are judicially translated into heaven. "All your aims must," therefore, "center in heaven, where reigns the Christ who has thus exalted you, enthroned on God's right hand. All your thoughts must abide in heaven, not on the earth. For, I say it once again, you have nothing to do with mundane things; you *died*—died once for all to the world; you are living another life. This life, indeed, is hidden now; it has no outward splendour as men count splendour; for it is a life with Christ, a life in God" *(Bishop Lightfoot)*. We shall seek that which we love and delight in. It is where our treasure is that our heart will be also. "Whom have I in heaven but thee? and there is none upon earth that I desire beside thee." What are the things we are seeking? Those things that are filling our thoughts and attracting our affections. It is upon these we set our wills and concentrate our energies. It is not difficult to seek what we love.

# JULY 31

*Endure hardness, as a good soldier of Jesus Christ.*—2 Tim. 2:3

"A good soldier," it has been said, "both abstains and sustains." This is to endure hardness. He has not only to fight in aggressive conflict, he has to withstand in defensive warfare. His power is seen far more in what he can *bear* than in what he can *do*. How true all this is spiritually! To be a good soldier of Jesus Christ we must know the discipline of laying aside every encumbrance, every weight, every entanglement. We must learn by actual experience how to "refuse," as well as how to accept. We lose as much often by yielding to the allurements of the world as by failing to claim the provisions of grace. The "hardness" that is essential to a "good soldier" can be brought about only by the discipline of trial, and fidelity to this law of the kingdom, that we "please him who hath chosen" us to be His soldiers. Character is formed by conduct, and conduct is the outcome of a living faith in a personal Savior. "Fight the good fight of faith."

# AUGUST 1

*The fruit of the Spirit is . . . faith.*—Gal. 5:22

Bishop Lightfoot observes "Faith seems not to be used here in its theological sense, 'belief in God.' Its position points rather to the passive meaning of faith, 'trustworthiness, fidelity, honesty,' " as in Matthew 23:23; Titus, 2:10; compare Romans 3:3. This virtue is the fruit of the Holy Spirit. It is as He dwells and reigns within that we shall bear this characteristic. Let us not seek to produce the fruit of godliness by the cultivation of ourselves or by imitating Christ's example, but rather by so honoring the Holy Spirit that He may produce in us and manifest through us the mind which was in Christ Jesus. The true imitation of Christ consists in the renunciation of ourselves, even as He ignored Himself, and living by faith on the Son of God, even as He lived by the Father. To be filled by the Spirit, and to be wholly under His gracious sway, is to be a fruitful branch.

# AUGUST 2

*The Lamb slain from the foundation of the world.*—Rev. 13:8

The Apostle John saw Christ under a twofold symbol. He saw Him as a Lion—"the Lion of the tribe of Juda" (Rev. 5:5). When we read of the lion we think of power and majesty. And this symbol fitly represents Christ, to whom all power in heaven and earth has been given. But it is power in seeming weakness. It is power in union with purity. He is also the Lamb—a little lamb, as the original denotes. "The Lamb slain," or, as in the fifth chapter, "as it had been slain." The wound marks are there, but it is not dead. It represents Him who, though He died, is alive for evermore; and yet the signs of suffering and death are visible. It is not the Lamb merely that is exalted —the lamb as a symbol of meekness, gentleness, and purity; but the lamb in connection with sacrifice—the lamb slain. It is not Christ the pure and holy One, the meek and self-sacrificing One, that is here represented, but Christ crucified. This is the sinner's plea: "He *died* for me." Our salvation is based on the eternal love of God as manifested in the gift of that sacrifice. It was from the foundation of the world.

## AUGUST 3

*His memory is on them that fear him.*—Luke 1:50

Three divine perfections are ascribed to God by the Virgin Mary in this hymn of praise. The first is *power*. In calling God "Almighty," she appears to make direct allusion to the expression of the angel—"the power of the Highest" (v. 35). Here is an act in which we have displayed the creative power of God. The second is *holiness:* "holy is his name" (v. 49). Mary had been brought to realize in a special way the holiness of the divine Being. The third divine perfection she dwells upon is *mercy*. She had already sung its praise in the words of the 48th verse, in relation to herself. She now celebrates God's mercy in a more general way, in relation to "them that fear him." This is not the fear of impenitent souls, but the fear of those who know God's forgiving grace; the fear of reconciled children, who are filled with a sense of His majesty and holiness and love. God's mercy rests on them. It abides on them "from generation to generation." It is a sense of that mercy that keeps the soul humble and broken in spirit. This is the true condition of heart to seek and abide in, if we would live in the fullness of God's blessing.

## AUGUST 4

*He said, It is finished: and he bowed his head, and gave up the ghost.*—John 19:30

As one has said, that saying, *It is finished,* "is but one word in the original; but in that one word is contained the sum of all joy, the very spirit of all Divine consolation" *(J. Flavel)*. What was it that Christ finished by His death? The fulfilling of the whole law; the making an end of sin. All the angels in heaven were not able, by their united strength, to lift that burden which Christ bore upon His shoulders, and "put away by the sacrifice of himself" (Heb. 9:26). This is the sum and substance of the glad tidings—Jesus had *finished* the work the Father had given Him to do. That work was the work of our salvation. It cost Him His life. He had come to accomplish this, knowing fully the nature of the sacrifice it would involve. He did it voluntarily. "Therefore doth my Father love me, because I lay down my life, that I might take it again. No man taketh it from me, but I lay it down of myself. I have power to lay it down, and I have power to take it again . . ." (John 10:17, 18).

# AUGUST 5

*Walk in newness of life.*—Rom. 6:4

Both life and liberty are needed before we are ready to "walk." The life is secured to us in Christ. He is our life. So too is liberty. Deliverance from sin's power, as well as from sin's penalty, is the fruit of Christ's death. "Stand fast therefore in the liberty wherewith *Christ hath made us free*" (Gal. 5:1). We are set free, not for idle contemplation or personal enjoyment, but for practical service. Walking in newness of life embraces the whole of that life that glorifies God. It is the apostle's favorite term for moral conduct. He says *"newness* of life," instead of *"new* life," because he would make prominent the idea of the new nature of this second life. The old life terminates at the cross. If we died with Christ, then the life that belongs to the "man of old" has been brought to an end; and if we are risen with Christ, we have entered into the life of the "new man." That is a life of freedom and of power. Walking in this life is not a hard, irksome struggle, but free, joyous action. What physical exercise is to the man in robust health, "walking in newness of life" is to the soul in the power of Christ's resurrection.

# AUGUST 6

*Whom the* Lord *loveth he correcteth.*—Prov. 3:12

The writer of the epistle to the Hebrews quotes from this passage. He "perceived and pointed out a tender meaning in the form of the expression 'My Son.'" That formula occurs often in the Proverbs, and a careless reader would pass it as a thing of course. Not so this inspired student of the Scripture: he gathers a meaning from the form of the word, before he begins to deal with its substance; the exhortation, he says, "speaketh unto you as unto children." Then, if we are His children, we must interpret all His dealings through this relationship—He is a Father to us. If He afflicts us, let us not call them punishments, but chastisements. Let us neither "despise" them nor "faint" under them. They are wisely and lovingly ordered, and exactly suited to the end in view—"our profit." He who appoints the "correction" gives grace to enable us to benefit by it. The great thing is never to lose sight of the fact that we are in a *Father's* hands, that His chastening is for His children's good, and that all is ordered by a love that is unfailing and a wisdom that is infinite.

# AUGUST 7

*The Comforter, which is the Holy Ghost, whom the Father
   will send in my name.*—John 14:26

"The Comforter" is one of the names of the third Person
of the Trinity. It is found only in John's gospel and first
epistle (14:16, 26; 15:26; 16:7; 1 John 2:1). The meaning of the word is "one who is called to another's side to aid
him," as an advocate in a court of justice. The Holy Spirit is,
therefore, represented as an Advocate or Counsel, "who suggests true reasonings to our minds and true courses of action
for our lives, who convicts our adversary, the world, of
wrong, and pleads our cause before God our Father. It is to
be noted that *Jesus* as well as the Holy Spirit is represented
as Paraclete. The Holy Spirit is to be *another* Paraclete, and
this falls in with the statement in the First Epistle: 'We have
an *Advocate* with the Father, Jesus Christ the righteous' "
*(Dr. Vincent).* Christ has not ceased to be our Comforter
because He has sent "another Comforter." Nor is He an
absent Advocate because His visible presence is withdrawn. The Holy Spirit fulfills His office of Comforter in
many ways, but chiefly in revealing the fact that the risen
Lord is verily *with,* and *in,* us.

# AUGUST 8

*The path of the just is as the shining light, that shineth more
   and more unto the perfect day.*—Prov. 4:18

Who are the just? The just are those who are justified.
And the justified are those who stand accepted in Christ's
merits. It is in Him, in whom we stand acquitted from
every charge, that we find the grace and life and power
to *desire* righteousness, to *work* righteousness, and to *live*
righteously. The path of such is compared to "the shining light, that shineth more and more unto the perfect
day." This is true of his experience, his enjoyment of salvation, his knowledge of God, and of his likeness to
Christ. Reference is here made to the rising sun. The man
who is traveling to meet the sun finds that each step he
takes brings him nearer and nearer to the source of all
light. Progress is a law of the spiritual life, in its true,
normal condition. We may count therefore upon deeper
joys, greater power, closer fellowship, and life more
abundant as we pursue the walk of faith. It is "more and
more," not more or less, "unto the perfect day."

## AUGUST 9

*Thou art all fair, my love; there is no spot in thee.*—Song of
  Sol. 4:7

These are the Lord's words concerning His Church. He
views her in Himself. It is of the Church that the Lord
speaks in those words, "Thy renown went forth among
the heathen for thy beauty: for it was perfect through
my comeliness, which I had put upon thee, saith the Lord
GOD" (Ezek. 16:14). It was not the result of her own
efforts, nor was it, indeed, *her* comeliness in any sense,
but "*My* comeliness, saith the Lord God." In this position
of acceptance, her deformities of sin are removed. "There
is no spot on thee." She is not only free from defilement,
she is positively lovely and fair. "Thou art *all* fair."

"Christ Jesus has no quarrel with His Spouse. She
often wanders from Him, and grieves His Holy Spirit,
but He does not allow her faults to affect His love. He
sometimes chides, but it is always in the tenderest manner, with the kindest intentions: it is 'My love' even then.
... It is well for us it is so, for if Jesus were as mindful
of injuries as we are, how could He commune with us?"

## AUGUST 10

*I pray not that thou shouldest take them out of the world,
  but that thou shouldest keep them from the evil.*—John
  17:15

Have we ever wondered why the Lord should leave His
children here on earth, when He has saved them from
so many dangers and snares? It might have seemed best
that He should at once remove them from scenes of such
painful conflict and alluring temptations. But our Lord has
a gracious purpose in keeping them for a season still in
the world. "I pray not that thou shouldest take them out
of the world." What would the world do without Christ's
witnesses on the earth? I pray, the Lord says, "that thou
shouldest keep them from the evil," and emphatically
from the *evil one*. It is he who is behind all temptations,
who is the worker in every subtle plot. "That *thou shouldest* keep them." Blessed is the man who is thus divinely
kept. We cannot keep ourselves. "The *Lord* is thy keeper." How slow some of us are in learning that fact. This
is the privilege of every blood-bought soul—to be "kept
by the power of God through faith unto salvation."

## AUGUST 11

*That through death he might destroy him that had the power of death, that is, the devil.*—Heb. 2:14

The battle scene of Christ's victory over Satan is not the temptation in the wilderness, but Calvary. It was "through death" that He conquered the prince of darkness. Not by almighty power, but "by his death." "Jesus suffering death overcame; Satan wielding death succumbed" *(Bengel).* As David cut off Goliath's head with the giant's own sword, so Christ, through death, vanquished him who had the power of death—that is, the devil.

The word "destroy" here is the same word we have in Romans 6:6: "That the body of sin might be destroyed." Satan is not annihilated—he is not in that sense destroyed. But his power is gone. He cannot overcome those who are entrenched in Christ.

These words put before us one only of the many purposes Christ had in His death. What He died to secure for us, as far as it bears on our present life, we may at once appropriate by faith. To the believer death has lost its power. Satan may terrify, but he cannot injure the soul by the terrors of death.

## AUGUST 12

*The Lord will not cast off for ever: but though he cause grief, yet will he have compassion.*—Lam. 3:31, 32

True repentance is never without hope, and hope rests, not on what we promise to do, but upon what God is, and has undertaken to accomplish. In the midst of the sorest chastisements the broken and contrite soul may take to itself this consolation, that "the Lord will not cast off for ever." All God's dealings with His erring children are wrought in the spirit of tenderest compassion. He has no pleasure in afflicting us; He chastises us for our profit.

It has been said truly, "It is certain there will be no patience, except there be hope. ... As patience cherishes hope, so hope is the foundation of patience; and hence consolation is, according to Paul, connected with patience. 'For whatsoever things were written aforetime were written for our learning, that we, through patience and comfort of the Scriptures, might have hope.' "

"Why art thou cast down, O my soul? and why art thou disquieted within me? hope in God: for I shall yet praise him ... (Ps. 43:5).

## AUGUST 13

*He hath prepared for them a city.*—Heb. 11:16

This is one of the many things which we are told God has prepared for His people. The Gospel is spoken of under the figure of a feast ready for the guests. "I have *prepared* my dinner" (Matt. 22:4). To those who enter into His glory He says, "Inherit the kingdom *prepared* for you from the foundation of the world" (Matt. 25:34).

Then we read, "Eye hath not seen, nor ear heard, neither have entered into the heart of man, the things which God hath *prepared* for them that love him. But God hath revealed them unto us by his Spirit" (1 Cor. 2:9, 10).

And so, in connection with our daily walk, how wonderful it is to learn that we have been "created in Christ Jesus unto good works, which God hath before [*prepared*] that we should walk in them" (Eph. 2:10).

In whichever direction the soul looks it finds that God's wisdom, and love, and power have been exercised on its behalf. In the past, the atoning sacrifice has been "prepared." In the future, our habitation has been prepared. "He hath prepared for them a city."

## AUGUST 14

*The joy of the LORD is your strength.*—Neh. 8:10

What is this joy? It is *divine*. There is a joy of youth, of circumstances, of prosperity. But the joy of the Lord rises above all these. Its source is heavenly, its nature is divine. It is the joy of *the Lord*. And so we can understand why it is an *abiding* joy. It does not come and go, but continues. "That my joy might *remain* in you" (John 15:11). Hence the apostle could say, "Rejoice in the Lord *always*." "As sorrowful, yet *always* rejoicing." It is a *satisfying* joy. One of the characteristics of all earthly joy is its unsatisfying nature. But the Lord's joy not only calms the mind, it fills the heart. Then it is a joy of great *practical* value. It is the secret of power for service. "The joy of the LORD is your *strength*." For *testimony*. It is when the heart is full of joy that the mouth can speak. The life itself then has a witness apart from our words. For *suffering*. It is when there is joy within that we can endure patiently. For *temptation*. Not simply in the sense of trial, but of allurements. When the heart is satisfied with the Lord's joy it will not be drawn aside by the world.

# AUGUST 15

*The God of peace ... make you perfect in every good work to do his will*—Heb. 13:20, 21

An inspired prayer offered on behalf of those who were already Christians. What was the subject of the prayer? That God would make them perfect. Perfect in what sense? Was it perfect as to their standing, their position of acceptance in God? No; for that was already true. In God's sight they were absolutely righteous—perfect in Christ Jesus. Was it that they might there and then become sinlessly perfect? No; for the word "perfect" here does not point to any such condition. The simple meaning of the word is to adjust, to fit, to put into joint. It supposes a condition of spiritual dislocation, so to speak. There was need of being brought into harmony with God —in their thoughts, in their affections, and in their wills. It was not a question touching their *position* or judicial standing, but a question touching their *condition*. This adjustment of their inner being was not the result of growth or of a life of holy obedience, but the essential condition of all this. It is only when they were thus made "perfect" that they could do His will.

# AUGUST 16

*The house that is to be builded for the* LORD *must be exceeding magnifical.*—1 Chron. 22:5

Solomon's Temple was a striking and beautiful type of Church of Christ. Whether we think of its foundation, its superstructure, or of what is related touching its construction, we shall find much to suggest deep spiritual teaching. It was built, not for David's, nor for Solomon's, but for God's glory. And so the spiritual building, of which all believers form a part, is intended to show forth the glory of God. It is "that now unto the principalities and powers in heavenly places might be known by the church the manifold vision of God" (Eps. 3:10). It shall be seen in the day of the Lord's appearing, when He comes "to be glorified in his saints, and to be admired in all them that believe," that this Temple, which is His body, is "exceeding magnifical."

What an honor to be a living stone built into this "house of God"! It is this building that is now in course of construction. It is growing "unto an holy temple in the Lord."

## AUGUST 17

*Pray one for another, that ye may be healed.*—James 5:16

The prayer here referred to is to be preceded by confession. Confession, not to the priest as Rome teaches, but confession "one to another." This is desirable, when we have *wronged* our neighbor, for instance; or when, under trouble, we seek *counsel* of a godly minister or friend; or when we seek an interest in the prayers of God's people. And, under certain circumstances, open confession of sin before the Church is desirable as a means of seeking God's forgiveness.

God's Word clearly encourages prayer for the body as well as the soul. "That ye may be healed," is the end to be sought. Though we cannot put "sickness" in the same category as sin, we know that bodily diseases are the effects of sin. Had sin never come into the world, it seems clear there would have been no sickness. We may pray for those that are sick; we may pray that they may be healed. We are exhorted to pray in faith, and we are told "the prayer of faith shall save the sick."

But there is another healing of which many of God's children stand in need, and that is *spiritual* healing.

## AUGUST 18

*What God is there in heaven or in earth, that can do according to thy works, and according to thy might?*—Deut. 3:24

Moses in this passage recognizes the fact that God had "begun to show" to him His greatness and His might. What he had seen of God's power and glory were but tokens of far greater manifestations of His majesty. It is his desire to go in and possess the land. "I pray thee, let me go over, and see the good land that is beyond Jordan." But it was not God's will that he should enter it. The words of our text are a part of the appeal that Moses made to God at this solemn stage of his life. He acknowledges the omnipotence of Jehovah. He contrasts Him with the gods of the heathen. The supremacy of Jehovah is the ground of all his confidence and hope.

There are times in the believer's life when he needs to give himself time to grasp more firmly what he has already received. There are times which he needs to spend in believing rather than in trying to understand—times of soliloquy, when he tells his soul what he knows already intellectually, but needs to appropriate spiritually.

## AUGUST 19

*As he which hath called you is holy, so be ye holy in all manner of conversation.*—1 Pet. 1:15

God is both our model and the power by which we rise toward that model. He is holy, and He has called us to Himself. We, too, therefore must be holy. By our regeneration and conversion we are set apart to God. That setting apart to Him makes us holy as to our calling. But we must be holy now "in all manner of conversation." The influence of His holiness must be seen in our outward conduct and course of life. We are holy only in so far as we are brought into contact with the center of all holiness. God has called us, not merely out of the darkness, but into the light—to Himself. It is only because of this we can be holy. Whatever He takes possession of becomes holy. When He took possession of the bush and dwelt in it, that bush became a "holy bush." It was God Himself who made it holy. So, when He calls us to Himself, and takes possession of us, we become a holy temple to God. He transfigures the outer life by renewing the mind, and this by filling our whole being with Himself.

## AUGUST 20

*God is not a man, that he should lie; neither the son of man, that he should repent.*—Num. 23:19

The faithfulness and immutability of God are attributes of His Character which give unspeakable comfort to the trusting soul. "If we believe not, yet he abideth faithful: he cannot deny himself" (2 Tim. 2:13). "He *abideth* faithful." He continues true to His own character, for "He is the same yesterday, and to-day, and for ever." This is the ground of hope in time of sore trial or temptation. "God is faithful" (1 Cor. 10:13) is the reason given why at such seasons we should never be shaken as to our expectation of deliverance. But let us not lose sight of the other side of the truth. He is just as faithful in His threatenings as in His promises. He remains ever true to Himself (James 1:17). All His gracious undertakings on behalf of His people are bound up inseparably with these great attributes of His character. It is for His own name's sake, therefore, that we can ask Him to fulfill His promises. God's own glory is involved in the matter. It has so pleased Him thus to link our spiritual good with the manifestation of His glory.

## AUGUST 21

*Thou art my portion, O* LORD.—Ps. 119:57

How little we know of all that is included in "God's unspeakable gift"! We are not only saved from eternal death by the reception of that gift—we are enriched by it. We become possessed of all things in it. The fullness of grace and of glory that gift contains is intended to meet every need of the soul as it arises. If I am conscious of needs not met, it is for me to discover by His Holy Spirit the divine provision in Him that will meet those needs. *"Thou art* my portion, O Lord." Not His sacraments, or His Word, or His Church, but Himself. The soul is in a bad condition when we begin to think we have not all in Christ—when we entertain the idea that something more in addition is needed. What is really needed is the removing of that which obscures our vision. To see Him clearly by faith is to be satisfied. "They shall be abundantly satisfied with the fatness of thy house" (Ps. 36:8). That "house" is Christ. They shall "overflow" with what they discover in Him.

## AUGUST 22

*None of us liveth to himself, and no man dieth to himself.*
—Rom. 14:7

Paul is here writing on certain questions connected with abstinence and the observance of days. He shows how, in all these things, there must be mutual toleration, and that each individual is responsible directly to the Lord. And now, in this seventh verse, he states the principle on which our conduct in these matters should be based.

He assumes that as Christians we all recognize the lordship of Christ over us. "To 'live to himself' is here, manifestly, not so much to live a *'selfish'* life as to live a life in which the mere dictates of conscience and will are the supreme rule, irrespective of Christ. 'None of us believers can make *anything lower* than Christ and His will the rule of life. Opinions, convictions, conscience itself, must be brought for light and correction to Him; for we are His.' Strictly speaking, this is a digression, as the main purport of the passage is to insist on the lawful freedom of believers with regard to *one another"* (Bishop Moule).

"Let no man seek his own, but every man another's wealth" (1 Cor. 10:24).

# AUGUST 23

*I have loved thee with an everlasting love: therefore with lov-
ing-kindness have I drawn thee.*—Jer. 31:3

Underneath everything that revelation makes known to
man is the fact of God's free sovereign love. It is the
source of every other blessing. It is impossible to go back
beyond the point of God's love to man. We can find
nothing in man himself *why* God should love him. All
we can do is to recognize the *fact* that it is so.

The believer sees it is an unchanging love, because it
is "everlasting." He may rely on this, that whatever circumstances of trial, of suffering, or of perplexity he may
be called to pass through, that love remains the same.

Then, again, he sees that God's love individualizes His
children. He says, "I have loved *thee*." As if there were
no others on whom to bestow His loving-kindness. This
personal aspect of God's love is not only very comforting,
it is also very humbling. To live in the rays of that love
is to have the natural hardness of our hearts melted and
all the bitterness removed. But another thing—this divine
love attracts the soul to Him who is the embodiment of
love: "With loving-kindness have I *drawn* thee."

# AUGUST 24

*I know their sorrows.*—Exod. 3:7

God was not dependent upon the complaints of the people
for his knowledge of their troubles. When He came down to
meet Moses at Horeb, He said, "I know their sorrows."
There is unspeakable comfort in the thought in time of
peculiar trial, "Well, He *knows* all about it." Even before
the deliverance comes, a sense of relief is found in knowing that He knows.

Sorrow is not sin, though it has come into the world in
consequence of sin. With sin Christ can have no sympathy, but He was the "man of sorrows, and acquainted
with grief" (Isa. 53:3). He is therefore "touched with the
feeling of our infirmities" (Heb. 4:15).

Every varying circumstance in life is a fresh occasion
for a deeper knowledge of the Lord Jesus Christ. We cannot learn the precious truths of the tenderness of His
humanity without passing through times of deep suffering in which His divine sympathy is needed and realized. Such occasions are the peculiar opportunities which
God gives us to know Him in a still deeper sense. He is never
nearer His people than when they are suffering for His sake.

# AUGUST 25

*Look unto the rock whence ye are hewn, and to the hole of the pit whence ye are digged.*—Isa. 51:1

Dr. Kay observes on this passage: "Whence were those living stones quarried, of which the house of Israel was built? Was it from one who was as 'good as dead' (Heb. 11:12; Rom. 4:19), and from his aged and barren consort? As an outward historical fact, it was; in reality, it could not be so. *Really* their origin was the plenitude of creative power.... Let not Zion, then—seemingly barren (49:21) —despond. She shall be fruitful (54:1). Let the faithful imitate him, who in that hour of darkness on Moriah 'stayed himself upon his God' (50:10), and thereby became 'heir of the world' (Roman. 4:13)."

The lesson to be learned from the text is trust in God. Small beginnings and adverse conditions are nothing with Him. He can use not only the "weak" and the "despised," but even the "things that are not," and bring out of them marvelous results. The wonders God has done in the past He is able and willing to accomplish in the future. What He needs of us is an unwavering faith and obedience. Let us not doubt His love or limit His power.

# AUGUST 26

*Thou shalt make a plate of pure gold, and grave upon it, like the engravings of a signet.*—Exod. 28:36

Josephus tells us that the headdress of the high priest was "a sort of crown, made of thick linen swathes" (Antiq. iii. 7, § 3). The color was white, and the only ornament on it was the "plate of pure gold," with its blue ribbon or fillet. The plate had engraved on it the inscription, "Holiness to the Lord." It was a type of the essential holiness of the Lord Jesus Christ. His was a life of holy separation to God. And it is written, "It shall be *always* upon *His* forehead, that *they* may be accepted before the Lord." This shows us how and why we are accepted. Not because of any holiness imparted to us; not in virtue of what we are, or have become by divine grace, but because of what He is. He is "always" in the presence of God for us. Are we ever tempted to think that because of fluctuating feelings and harassing doubts we are no longer acceptable to God? Let us remember that it is never because of anything in us that we are accepted at all. The measure of our acceptance is what Christ is to God; and that remains ever the same.

# AUGUST 27

*Thy word is a lamp unto my feet, and a light unto my path.*
—Ps. 119:105

The two parts of this verse are not two different ways of saying the same thing. They point to the varying circumstances of life through which the child of God has to make his journey. At night the Word of God is the lamp to the feet; in the day, that Word is the sun to his path.

Sometimes his path lies through thick darkness, but, like the lantern held close to the feet, God's Word always gives sufficient light for the next step. And in times of freedom from perplexity or difficulty, the Word of God, like the sun in the heavens, is the secret of life's true sunshine.

But in order that the Word of God may be indeed our lamp and our light, we must make it our daily and diligent study. We must "take heed to it, as unto a light that shineth in a dark place." We must submit our beings to its searching, cleansing, and illuminating influences. We must be obedient to its gentle admonitions; we must not hinder it in its reproving, warning, and comforting work. The paths along which it will lead us will always be "paths of righteousness," of holiness, and of peace.

# AUGUST 28

*The accuser of our brethren is cast down, which accused them before our God day and night.*—Rev. 12:10

This is one of the names that God's Word gives to our great spiritual adversary. Not all accusations of which we are conscious come from him, because conscience, unless it is utterly seared, has to fulfill this office. When we do wrong conscience accuses. But even when the conscience is "void of offence," Satan will often do all he can to harass the soul of the believer. He will accuse even when God has accepted us, but he cannot condemn. It is this we are told that he does "before our God day and night." "Who shall lay any thing to the charge of God's elect? It is God that justifieth. Who is he that condemneth? It is Christ that died, yea rather, that is risen again, who is even at the right hand of God, who also maketh intercession for us" (Rom. 8:33, 34).

The secret of successfully meeting this great enemy we have in the verse that follows our text: "And they overcame him by the blood of the Lamb, and by the word of their testimony."

# AUGUST 29

*Whoso trusteth in the* LORD, *happy is he.*—Prov. 16:20

We never know the meaning of trust until we learn the nature of trial. It is in the trial that we have to put into practice the theory of beliving in God. Trust is to become the habit of the soul. But often the young disciple is greatly perplexed about faith, because, instead of being occupied with the object of faith, he is thinking of the act of believing. But faith never comes in this way. It has no existence apart from Him who is the object of it. "Whoso trusteth *in the* LORD." Let our thoughts be occupied with God's revealed character, with what He is to us and what He has done for us, and we shall, without *trying* to believe, begin to put our trust in Him. It is with what God is that we have to be occupied. The mind then finds its resting place. It stays itself on God. A peace is then known that could never be found in the world. We see then how true are the words, "Happy is he."

Trial therefore is the school of trust. It is there we learn the lesson of implicitly confiding in God, and of waiting patiently on Him.

# AUGUST 30

*The king held out ... the golden sceptre.... So Esther drew near, and touched the top of the sceptre.*—Esth. 5:2

"Esther was not acting 'according to law' (ch. 4:16) in now drawing near. She did it at the peril of her life. We picture her waiting for the king's notice with tearful eye and trembling heart, lest the 'golden sceptre' (v. 2) should not be held out to her. Our great and gracious King is accessible to the meanest of His subjects at any moment. There is indeed a Mediator (1 Tim. 2:5) between Him and us, but through Him we may come 'at all times.' *His* throne on which He sits is a throne of grace. His sceptre is one of boundless beneficence. We may touch it when we will (v. 3). If He rebukes us, it is not for coming when He does not send; it is for not coming oftener than we do. ... The king of Persia made promise to Esther in very 'royal' fashion; he offered her, in word, much more than he had any intention of granting. 'It shall be given thee to the half of the kingdom.' God's promises are according to His wisdom as well as His love, and they rest on His faithfulness as well as His mercy."

# AUGUST 31

*The free gift is of many offences unto justification.*—Rom. 5:16

"We may paraphrase these words. The Gift, in wonder and greatness of quality, far exceeds the Ruin, though each is the result of one person's act (for, as we know, the sentence and execution *was* the result of one man's one sin, while the atonement and justification is the result, in a sense, of many men's many sins). I say the Gift exceeds the Ruin; for, while the result of Adam's sin was just the lawful reign of death over *men* as sinners, the result of Christ's work shall be not a mere reversal of this, but the reign of *justified men* over death in glory" *(Bishop Moule)*.

"With *'the offence* of one' (v. 15) he has contrasted the grace of God and of Jesus Christ in its double fulness. Now, with the one sinner, in the first case, he contrasts the *multitude* of sinners who are the *objects* of justification in the second. What a difference between the power of the spark which sets fire to the forest by lighting a withered branch, and the power of the instrument which extinguishes the conflagration at the moment when every tree is on fire, and makes them all alive again!" *(Godet)*.

## SEPTEMBER 1

*The fruit of the Spirit is . . . meekness*—Gal. 5:23

The apostle had before spoken of the *works* of the flesh; now he says the *fruit* of the Spirit. "This change is significant. The flesh is a rank weed which produces no fruit, properly so called (compare Eph. 5:9-11, Rom. 6:21); and St. Paul's language here recalls the contrast of the fig and vine with the thorn and the thistle in the parable (Matt. 7:16, *seq.*)" *(Bishop Lightfoot)*.

Meekness fits us to receive instruction, disposes us to refrain from feeling angry under provocation, and to forgive injuries. Meekness will enable us cheerfully to submit to God's will, however trying the circumstances. Meekness does not mean a weak, yielding disposition. True Christian meekness is perfectly compatible with a strong will and a decided character. The man who is really meek lives in submission to Christ as his supreme Lord. The Holy Ghost is the Spirit of Christ, and meekness is one of the most striking features of the mind of Christ. Let that Holy Spirit dwell in you, let Him abide as the reigning Lord within the soul, and meekness will be a sure outcome of His presence.

## SEPTEMBER 2

*Wait on the* LORD: *be of good courage, and He shall strengthen thine heart.*—Ps. 27:14

We are often waiting *for* the Lord, as if He were not willing or ready to bless, when all the while we should rather wait *on* the Lord, because He is waiting to be gracious to us. To wait on the Lord is to seek His face, to hear His voice, to contemplate His character. There is no circumstance in life in which we may not continue in this attitude of restful confidence and holy expectation.

None ever waited upon the Lord in vain. Let us encourage ourselves, not in our attainments or successes, but in the Lord. It is He who shall strengthen our hearts.

There is a promise to this effect: "They that wait on the LORD shall renew their strength" (Isa. 40:31). That is, they shall *change* their strength. They shall have it perpetually renewed. It will be continually, grace instead of grace. And in another sense it is also true. They shall give up their own strength and take God's in exchange. That is a strength which shall never disappoint. It is not followed by exhaustion, and it can never run out.

## SEPTEMBER 3

*Neither shall there be leaven seen with thee in all thy quarters.*
—Exod. 13:7

It was not enough for the Israelite to say he was not aware that there was any leaven in his dwelling; he had to make diligent search. Not until that search had been honestly made could he rest in the consciousness that, so far as he knew, he was clear from its presence. So it must be with us, who would be honest in our consecration to God. We may say, "I am not conscious that there is anything I am withholding from God. I am not conscious of keeping anything that is displeasing to Him." But the first point is: Have I made diligent search? Have I come to God and honestly asked Him to search me? There may be recesses in my being which I know have not been brought under the penetrating power of His holy light. There may be corners in which "doubtful things" are still lurking, and which would no longer be doubtful, if I honestly asked God to show me His will concerning them. The fear lest such a surrender of one's being would involve a complete clearing out of a multitude of things may still be keeping the soul in a state of partial consecration (1 Cor. 5:6, 7).

## SEPTEMBER 4

*Sit still, my daughter.*—Ruth 3:18

Stillness of soul is what the great majority of God's children need. Restlessness in Christian service is often mistaken for activity and zeal. The reason of the exhaustion so many experience in working for the Lord is to be found in the lack of inward rest. Perhaps it is one of the last things we think we ought to do, when we first enter upon His service, namely, to let ourselves down, with all our cares, and rest in His Almighty arms. And yet it is one of the first lessons the Good Shepherd constrains His following sheep to learn. "The LORD is my shepherd; I shall not want. He *maketh me to lie down* in green pastures: he leadeth me beside waters [of *quietness*]." Before we can work without friction, without exhaustion, and without waste of strength, He teaches us to be *still*. He sets us free from the energy of the flesh, and from the fret and disquietude of the natural man.

Here, again, is the secret of all progress in our knowledge of God: "Be still, and know that I am God" (Ps. 46:10). "Mary . . . sat at Jesus' feet, and heard his word" (Luke 10:39).

## SEPTEMBER 5

*As the body is one, and hath many members . . . so also is Christ.*—1 Cor. 12:12

When we have seen the meaning of substitution (Christ *for* me), we have to go on and learn the meaning of union (I in Christ and Christ *in* me). We have to understand what this mystical union is in relation to ourselves individually, and in relation to believers collectively. Christ "is the head of the body, the church" (Col. 1:18). There can be only one Head, but there are many members. Each member recognizes that Head, and is under the control of that Head. There is but one Center of wisdom and of will, and but one Source of life and of power. That Center and that Source is Christ. But Christ is not only the name that belongs to Head—the man Christ Jesus. It is the name that belongs also to the members. All believers are included under that name. As the natural human body is one, so "also is Christ," i.e., the mystical body, of which the risen Lord is the Head.

A true apprehension of our relationship to Him as the Head will bring us to a right knowledge of our relation to the members.

## SEPTEMBER 6

*Let us lift up our heart with our hands unto God in the heaven.*—Lam. 3:41

The lifting up of the hands to God was a part of worship in the Old Testament ritual. It was an act of adoration. David says, "Let . . . the lifting up of my hands [be] as the evening sacrifice" (Ps. 141:2). It was the expression of earnest importunate supplication. "I stretch forth my hands unto thee" (Ps. 143:6). But no mere outward sign was acceptable to God apart from its spiritual reality. So here we read, "Let us lift up our *heart* with our hands." David often speaks of lifting up his *soul* to God. "Unto Thee, O LORD, do I lift up my soul" (Ps. 25:1). That was expressive of a real spiritual approach. It was no mere formal act of worship. It was a proof of sincerity. He uses it as a sort of argument in prayer. "Cause me to know the way wherein I should walk; *for* I lift up my soul unto thee" (Ps. 143:8).

Let us see that we remember the necessity of both of these parts in all prayer—the outward act of reverence and the inward reality of the spirit. Let the body as well as the soul be engaged in all our acts of worship.

## SEPTEMBER 7

*Rejoicing in hope.*—Rom. 12:12

True hope is not a vague wish, touching that which is uncertain. It is a combination of desire and expectation. There may be desire without expectation, and there may be expectation without desire. In neither case have we real hope. When we hope, we both desire and expect that for which we hope. The hope of the Church is emphatically Christ in His coming glory.

We cannot know what Christian hope is until we know what it is to trust in Christ. Many are hoping in the forgiveness of sins, as if pardon depended upon something yet to be accomplished. But the apostle regards this as a present possession to be grasped by faith (Eph. 1:7). We *believe* in the forgiveness of sins, and we *hope* for our complete conformity to Christ at His coming. "We shall be like him: for we shall see him as he is" (1 John 3:2). "And every man that hath this hope in him"—"this hope," that is, the hope of His appearing, and of our being made like Him—"purifieth himself, even as he is pure." This glorious prospect, in proportion as it is realized, will fill the soul with joy, "rejoicing in hope."

## SEPTEMBER 8

*Thou art weighed in the balances, and art found wanting.*
—Dan. 5:27

Such was the Lord's message to Belshazzar through His servant Daniel. The words should be read in connection with the 23rd verse: "The God in whose hand thy breath is, and whose are all thy ways, hast thou not glorified." Here is the standard by which men's hearts and lives are to be judged. Every life will be found wanting which has not for its end the glory of God. It is not a question as to whether we have committed few or many sins, small or great transgressions. A life may be moral, according to the highest earthly standard, and yet be sadly wanting when weighed in the balances of the sanctuary.

God has called us, not only out of darkness into light, out of death into life, but out of a course of self-seeking into a life which has for its end "the praise of the glory of his grace" (Eph. 1:6).

Self is the center of every life that has never come under the renewing power of God's grace. It may be strictly moral, and even religious, but it will be essentially self-centered until the great change has taken place.

## SEPTEMBER 9

*He hath filled the hungry with good things; and the rich he hath sent empty away.*—Luke 1:53

The "hungry" and the "rich" are the two classes into which men generally may be divided—those who feel their need, and are ready to receive; and those who are self-satisfied, and have no desire to be blessed. The words apply not to those only who are outside the kingdom; in a certain sense they are applicable to many who are within that city whose walls are salvation. It is possible for a truly converted soul to relapse into a condition of such deadness and worldly conformity that the description given of the Laodicean Church may be true of him: "Thou sayest, I am rich, and increased with goods, and have need of nothing; and knowest not that thou art wretched, and miserable, and poor, and blind, and naked" (Rev. 3:17).

Lack of desire for heavenly food, like want of appetite for the bread that perishes, is a symptom of declining health, and the forerunner of greater evils. The soul that does not come receptive will go away empty. "Open thy mouth wide, and I will fill it" (Ps. 81:10).

## SEPTEMBER 10

*I will give them one heart, and one way, that they may fear me for ever, for the good of them, and of their children after them.*—Jer. 32:39

These words are prophetic of Israel, and refer to their restoration. The connection between their inner condition and outward conduct is shown here. They cannot be "one" as to their "way" unless they are "one" as to their "heart." By "heart" we must understand that central part of our being where three things are focussed—the thoughts, the emotions, and the will. God is able to bring these three parts of our being into complete submission to Himself. The "heart" often gets wrong, even after we have been born from above and have the new nature; and when the "heart" is wrong, the "way" gets wrong. This, then, must be our constant prayer: "Lord, put my heart right. Keep it right, and then shall I glorify Thee in my way."

"Teach me, thy way, O LORD; I will walk in thy truth: unite my heart to fear thy name" (Ps. 86:11).


## SEPTEMBER 11

*Be not conformed to this world: but be ye transformed by the renewing of your mind.*—Rom. 12:2

These words of exhortation must be taken in connection with the words that precede: "I beseech you therefore, brethren, by the mercies of God, that ye present your bodies. . . ." This nonconformity to the spirit of the age can only follow when the consecration to God is real and complete. The world has its influence; and even the Christian is in danger of being drawn aside. Consecration therefore must be followed up by transformation. There must be a daily and continuous transfiguration of the pardoned soul into the image of Jesus Christ.

It is not by mere negative efforts to abstain from worldly pursuits and pleasures that we shall obey this exhortation but by obedience to the positive side—actual transformation *by the renewing of the mind.*

This implies that the believer makes use of the means of grace. He must read the Scriptures. He must prayerfully ponder over what God has revealed. He must seek to submit his whole being to their teaching and power.

## SEPTEMBER 12

*I have seen his ways, and will heal him.*—Isa. 57:18

Healing, in a spiritual sense, is often referred to in connection with the backslidings of His people whom God forgives. "Return, ye backsliding children, and I will heal your backslidings" (Jer. 3:22). The soul that seeks God's pardon truly is not content with mere forgiveness; it desires cleansing and healing. Not the guilt of sin only, but its defilement and power are sought when we are thoroughly in earnest about our soul's salvation. And it is this that God promises.

The cross of Christ is not the source of our pardon only, it is the place of our healing—*"With his stripes we are healed"* (Isa. 53:5). As we received pardon, so we receive healing. Both are the fruit of Christ's death, and both are accepted by faith. "Thy faith hath made thee whole" (Mark 5:34).

It is the whole soul, the soul that lives in spiritual health, that is alone ready to meet temptation. We fall before the allurements of sin, because temptation too often finds us enfeebled by disease—spiritual weakness.

Let us seek and claim that which God has bestowed upon us in Christ.

## SEPTEMBER 13

*If any man thirst, let him come unto me, and drink.*—John 7:37

To thirst is to feel a sense of need. The soul's necessities are here considered under the figure of natural or physical thirst. Christ had come into the world to meet man's deep need. He was the "fountain of living waters." He knew what was in man, and it is to man's deepest need that He appeals when He says, "If any man thirst, let him come unto me."

To come unto Him means the soul's approach in prayer. But we may come even though we utter no word in prayer. We draw nigh, we lie low at His feet, we look up into His face. We thank Him for calling us, for permitting us to take up our place before Him, with all our wants. How encouraging is His gracious declaration: "Whosoever drinketh of the water that I shall give him shall never thirst!" That is, he that is in the habit of drinking of that water finds that his thirst is continually being allayed. Lord, evermore give me this water.

## SEPTEMBER 14

*I, even I, am he that comforteth you.*—Isa. 51:12

God's dealings with Israel are a sample of His dealings not only with the Church, but with the individual believer. The fact of His condescension is the thought that underlies the form of the expression, "I, even I." Let your soul ponder that fact. It is the God of heaven and earth, the Creator and Sustainer of all things, who thus stoops tenderly to soothe the sorrowing and cast-down soul.

And when He gives comfort, who then can give trouble? It is a comfort that is superior to all outward surroundings. It is God's own peace in the heart, a peace, therefore, that passes all understanding (Phil. 4:7).

This comfort is no mere question of the emotions—it is intelligent. He gives us a reason for the comfort He administers. He shows us the ground on which our consolation rests. This reason and this ground are found in His revealed character, in His unchanging faithfulness, His all-sufficient power, His infinite resources, and in the exceeding greatness of His love. "Let not your heart be troubled: ye believe in God, believe also in me" (John 14:1).

## SEPTEMBER 15

*Sin shall not have dominion over you: for ye are not under the law, but under grace.*—Rom. 6:14

Sin is personified in this chapter, and is regarded as a master. He demands our service, and pays wages. "The wages of sin is death." But Christ has set us free from sin's claim. Sin no longer has any authority over us. Because Christ died, and we died with Him, sin has no legal right to lord it over us. We may therefore claim at once this our privilege of freedom from sin's dominion. It is not a question of feeling, but of faith. If we believe that this was the purpose of Christ's death, that sin should no longer be our master, and if we believe that Christ succeeded in attaining that purpose, then all we have to do is to appropriate by faith this our present privilege of continuous emancipation from sin's power. We are no longer under the law, which would mean that we were in a course which has for its goal this freedom. But we are under grace, which means that freedom is the starting point, that we run in this liberty, and not for it.

"If the Son therefore shall make you free, ye shall be free indeed" (John 8:36).

## SEPTEMBER 16

*The* LORD *pondereth the hearts.*—Prov. 21:2

Man judges by that which is visible and external. Hence he is often deceived. But "the LORD seeth not as man seeth; for man looketh on the outward appearance, but the LORD looketh on the heart" (1 Sam. 16:7). We read as a man "thinketh in his heart, so is he" (Prov. 23:7). Not as he speaks with his life, or even as he appears in his actions, but "as he thinketh in his heart." Because it is there that the man really lives. And what else is it that does act in man's heart? We may say, "as a man desires in his heart," or "as a man purposeth in his heart." The true condition of the man before God is what his heart is. Let that be right and the whole man is right. The Lord looks at our hearts. He deals with us in reference to our hearts.

To the soul that is unwilling to break with sin, this thought of God's omniscience is a perpetual source of misery. But to the believer, whose whole heart's desire is to please God, and to have Christ reigning supremely within, this is one of the most comforting facts of revelation.

## SEPTEMBER 17

*A bruised reed shall He not break.*—Matt. 12:20

These words are a quotation from Isaiah (42:3), and are applied by the evangelist to the Messiah. The prophet in that chapter gives a description of the Lord's servant. Here we have a view of His tenderness in His dealings with the humble and contrite. The figure brings out the gentleness and longsuffering of the Redeemer. Some interpret the words as referring to the shepherd's reed. Even the broken reed which can no longer give forth its musical note, and is therefore useless, the Good Shepherd will not destroy and cast away. He is able and willing to restore it. Others think allusion is made to the familiar reed that grew in marshy places, that bent with every gust of wind—the frail reed, the very symbol of weakness. A *broken* reed. What can be done with so useless a thing? The Lord Jesus will not cast away those who are thus represented in this figure. They are not beyond His power to restore. These are the very kind of people He has come to save. Broken and contrite hearts are those He delights to bind up and to heal. "He healeth the broken in heart, and bindeth up their wounds" (Ps. 147:3).

## SEPTEMBER 18

*Open thou mine eyes, that I may behold wondrous things out of thy law.*—Ps. 119:18

There are two veils that need to be removed before we can see the glory of God's grace—the veil that hides the truth, and the veil that covers our eyes. It is the Lord Himself who alone can remove these coverings. We live in the days of full Gospel light, because that which for ages was hidden has now been unveiled. As far as the truth is concerned, there is now no obscurity. "The darkness is past, and the true light now shineth" (1 John 2:8). And yet we may fail to see the light. We may see no beauty in Christ, and we may behold no wondrous things in His Word. Another veil needs to be removed. The risen Lord not only "opened to" those two sorrowing disciples "the Scriptures" (Luke 24:32), He also opened "their understanding, that they might understand the Scriptures" (v. 45). So the psalmist prays, "Open thou mine eyes, that I may behold wondrous things out of thy law." Let us never forget we need His enlightening grace each time we come to His holy Word.

## SEPTEMBER 19

*The God of all grace.*—1 Pet. 5:10

What an encouraging aspect of God's character is this! It is one of His names. The whole Gospel is comprehended in the names of God. He is the God of peace—the God of hope—the God of all comfort. Here we have "the God of all grace." Grace embraces our every need. "God is able to make all grace abound toward you" (2 Cor. 9:8). It is submission to His will, and trust in His love and faithfulness, that are needed on our part, in order to live in the stream of His boundless, ceaseless, and victorious grace. We none of us know what grace means, until we are brought to rely on God's pardoning love to us in Jesus Christ. Grace means unmerited favor—receiving what we do not deserve. Grace is the opposite of merit—we are saved by grace. But it also means the complement of our need—that which fills up the emptiness. It is on the ground of grace that God deals with us, not only when first we come to Him in our guilt and misery, but all along the way, and every day in our lives, when, as pardoned souls, and children in His family, we walk in the light of His countenance. We dare not leave this ground of grace.

## SEPTEMBER 20

*Happy is the man that findeth wisdom, and the man that get-teth understanding.*—Prov. 3:13

In the eighth chapter of Proverbs, Wisdom is no mere abstract quality, but a Person. It is none other than Christ Himself, who says, "Unto you, O men, I call; and my voice is to the sons of man" (8:4). "Blessed is the man that heareth me, watching daily at my gates, waiting at the posts of my doors. For whoso findeth me findeth life, and shall obtain favour of the LORD" (vv. 34, 35). Wisdom is thus embodied in the divine Person. To find wisdom is not something to be attained by human effort. It is to receive Him "Who of God is made unto us wisdom" (1 Cor. 1:30), and "in Whom are hid all the treasures of wisdom and knowledge" (Col. 2:3). To find Christ is to find life: this is true blessedness.

"Happy is the man that *findeth* wisdom." Every such man is *found* of Him who is Wisdom. As we find righteousness complete and perfect, when we find Christ, so we find in Him wisdom also. It is the office of the Holy Spirit to unveil to the heart and mind of the believer all those treasures of wisdom that are stored up in Him.


## SEPTEMBER 21

*We know that all things work together for good to them that love God.*—Rom. 8:28

A declaration that is especially comforting to the believer in times of perplexity and trial. There are seasons in one's life when all things seem to be against us. It is then that we need a divine assurance like this. Faith says, not "We hope," but "We know." This is one of the things of which the child of God is privileged to speak with a calm and steady assurance. "We know that all things *work together*." However dark and mysterious the outward aspect may be, let us not forget there is a divine purpose that is steadily being fulfilled. God's will of love is being done, and every event of life is contributing to its fulfillment. Let faith grasp that fact. All things are working together for my good. Life is like an elaborate piece of tapestry that is being woven on the loom. For the pattern to be beautiful the colors must not be all of one hue. While some must be bright and beautiful, others must be dark and somber. As they are worked together they all contribute to the beauty of the pattern.

## SEPTEMBER 22

*My meditation of him shall be sweet: I will be glad in the*
  LORD.—Ps. 104:34

Perhaps, in these busy days, what Christians need most is
the habit of devout meditation. There may be stated times
for prayer and Bible reading, and yet little or no meditation. It is in those quiet seasons of prayerful meditation,
over some fact or declaration of God's Word, that our
faith strikes its root down deep into the truth. Time is
needed to appropriate, personally, what is already ours in
Christ. It is in this way that our knowledge, which at the
first is elementary, though true and saving, becomes deep-
ened and developed. References to this fuller knowledge
are frequent in Paul's epistles. For the lack of it many of
God's children are weak and superficial. Our meditation,
if it is to be profitable, will be "of Him." He is the Center,
and Sum, of all revealed truth. (Song of Sol. 2:3).

By meditation too we sow the seeds for future action.
As out of the heart are the issues of life; so by meditation we lay up in our heart that word of life which will
occupy our thoughts, purify our desires, and direct our
wills (Jer. 15:16). We feed on the Word, and assimilate
it into our being.

## SEPTEMBER 23

*Our God hath not forsaken us.*—Ezra 9:9

This was Ezra's comfort in time of sore distress. He
mourns over the sad backslidings of his people; he seeks
to humble himself before God on account of Israel's sin;
and then goes on to add, "Our God hath not forsaken us
in our bondage, but hath extended mercy unto us" (v. 9).
In our deepest humiliations let us never doubt God's love
and mercy toward us. Because of our sins we deserve His
chastisements. But let us not forget that it is as a Father
that He deals with us (Heb. 12:7, 8).

To conclude that because of trial and suffering God hath
forsaken us is to yield to unbelief. And there is no sin that
is more displeasing to God. It aims a blow at the very
character of God, for it questions His trustworthiness.

"The LORD will not forsake his people for his great
name's sake . . ." (1 Sam. 12:22). These words were spoken
to Israel and apply primarily to them, but they are true of
God's spiritual Israel today. Let us stay ourselves upon the
unchanging character of our God. He cannot deny Himself
(Heb. 13:8).

## SEPTEMBER 24

*It is good for me to draw near to God.*—Ps. 73:28

God is the Center and the Source of all our happiness. We are privileged to draw near to Him in our unworthiness and sin, through His Son Jesus Christ. We draw nigh not merely for pardon and relief, but to find in Him our Portion, and in His presence our Home. The first thing He would have us do is to "draw near" to Him. He has opened the way and provided the sacrifice. Every barrier that stood in the way between the guilty sinner and the holy God, He Himself has removed by the blood of His cross. The way into the holiest has now been made plain (Heb. 10:19, 20, 22).

The believer is one who not only came to God at his conversion, but who is in the habit of coming continually unto Him. It is to such that those words in Heb. 7:25 primarily refer: He is able to be saving to the very end, those who are in the habit of coming to God by Jesus Christ. There can be no real act of worship without thus drawing near. We must enter into the *place* of worship—into the holiest of all—if we would know what worship means.

## SEPTEMBER 25

*Let patience have her perfect work, that ye may be perfect and entire, wanting nothing.*—James 1:4

The apostle refers in the passage to the trial of faith. God, who gives the faith, appoints the trial. The purpose of the trial is the strengthening of faith. But this is not reached if the trial does not have its full course. The endurance, which the trial calls for, must continue. It must have its "perfect work." The blessing hidden in the trial may never be realized, simply because the endurance did not last. Therefore it is that in every trial our special need is that of patience. And the secret of this patience is a spirit of submission to the will of God, and an unquestioning faith in His love. Judged by outward surroundings, the believer may sometimes look very much like one forsaken of God and afflicted. But faith works through all adverse circumstances, and keeps steadily in view the unchanging love and faithfulness of God.

The grace of God can enable a man not only to submit to the trial that God appoints; it can enable him to rise higher—namely, to acquiesce in it, and still higher, to *rejoice* in it. (See 2 Cor. 12:9.)

## SEPTEMBER 26

*A God of truth and without iniquity, just and right is He.*
—Deut. 32:4

It is not only on the mercy and love of God that we are privileged to rest. Every one of the divine attributes are full of comfort and encouragement to the soul that comes to God through Jesus Christ. But there is nothing that gives such "strong consolation" as the fact that He is "a God of truth." He is "a just God and a Saviour" (Isa. 45:21). But apart from the cross of Jesus Christ this revelation of the character of God cannot be found. It is only in the crucified One we see that "mercy and truth are met together," and that "righteousness and peace have kissed each other" (Ps. 85:10).

The Gospel is a manifestation of the righteousness of God. It shows us, as nothing else can, that God hates sin; that He could not pass it by unpunished, even when it was on His Son, only as an imputed thing. His standard of justice and holiness is not lower under the Gospel than under the law. He is none the less a God of judgment because He is the God of love. How firm therefore is the rock on which the soul stands who takes his place in Christ Jesus. (See Rom. 8:33).

## SEPTEMBER 27

*Humble yourselves therefore under the mighty hand of God, that he may exalt you in due time.*—1 Pet. 5:6

Rightly understood, these words teach us the secret of humility. How to be humble is the question that often presses upon us. We see its necessity; we admire the grace of humility; we desire ourselves to be humble. But how is it to be brought about? A power is needed greater than our own. It must be the power of God. It is in "the mighty hand of God." And how shall we get the benefit of that power? We must yield to it. In other words, we must get "under" it. We may become partakers of the power of evil by yielding to it. So it is by yielding to the power of God that we partake of that power. It is not by struggling or striving to make ourselves humble that we attain the grace of humility. We must cease from self, and submit to the power of God. The power that can alone bring us to the dust, and keep us there, resides in God, and not in us. We humble ourselves under His hand, when we are willing to take His will instead of our own.

## SEPTEMBER 28

*They shall put my name upon the children of Israel; and I will bless them.*—Num. 6:27

That name was a name of blessing. Wherever it rested it brought peace and prosperity to the soul. First, there was the blessing of His keeping power: "The LORD bless thee, and keep thee" (v. 24). Second, there was the blessing of a bright and joyous experience: "The LORD make his face shine upon thee, and be gracious unto thee"( v. 25). We need the sun*shine* as well as the sunlight of His grace. Third, there was the divine witness to the fact that God was well pleased: "The LORD lift up his countenance upon thee, and give thee peace" (v. 26). We use the phrase, "He gives His countenance to the matter," when we would express a man's approval of a thing. The blessing here described is that which Enoch enjoyed when it is said that "before his translation he had this testimony, that he pleased God" (Heb. 11:5). This witness brings to the soul a sweet peace that comes directly from God.

To have the blessing of God's name means that He to whom we belong has come and taken possession of us. (See Isa. 63:19).

## SEPTEMBER 29

*Hereby perceive we the love of God, because he laid down his life for us.*—1 John 3:16

The apostle does not say here the love of Christ, but the "love of God," although he says, "because he laid down his life for us." It is of Christ as God that the apostle writes. That love is the great power that melts the hardest heart, and draws even the most rebellious to His feet. We have to "perceive" it. When by God's grace we know and believe in that love the natural enmity of our hearts is expelled, and we are no longer aliens and strangers, but fellow citizens with the saints. The death of Christ is the expression of His deepest love. It was not for those who were His friends, but for "enemies" that He laid down His life. (Compare John 15:13 with Rom. 5:8).

God's love to us is not to end with us. God has called us to walk in love, and to dwell in love. And this love is not our love to God, but His own love. To dwell in that love is to dwell in God (1 John 4:16). This love is also to be in us as the motive-power of our lives. So our Lord prayed in behalf of His disciples. (See John 17:26).

# SEPTEMBER 30

*He knoweth the way that I take.*—Job 23:10

"He knoweth the way that is with me" (margin). To the child of God this fact is a source of comfort. God knows all the circumstances of my life, every detail of my daily path. He knows, too, the weakness and frailty of our nature (Ps. 103:14). This gives no excuse for our sinning, but it is a ground for His compassion. If we take the place of the helpless and dependent, He will undertake for us. He will be our wisdom in the matter of guidance. He will be our strength in the matter of duty and difficulty. He will be everything to us that our circumstances demand.

But if, on the other hand, we are self-complacent as to the uprightness of the way that we take, we shut ourselves off from all the provisions of His grace. The ruling principle of our life is then self, rather than Christ. God has not called us to Himself that we should be our own guides, or our own masters. The true life is the life of self-renunciation—the life that hangs entirely upon God and expects Him to supply every need. It is in the sphere of our conscious weakness that divine strength is perfected.

# OCTOBER 1

*The fruit of the Spirit is ... temperance.*—Gal. 5:22

This does not mean "temperance" in the sense in which the word is ordinarily used, but "self-control"; that is, the control of the whole man. Not that we are able to control ourselves. But if the Holy Ghost, who is *in* the believer, is honored and obeyed, He will bring forth His fruit. And included in that fruit is this grace of divine government. We grieve the Spirit not merely by yielding to evil habits, but by allowing those tendencies of our nature which are not sinful in themselves to pass beyond their legitimate bounds. When this fruit of temperance is the characteristic of the man, all the powers and energies of his renewed being are divinely regulated. That which distinguishes Christianity from the highest attainments of pagan morality is this: that while in the latter we find *self* enthroned, in the former it is *Christ* who takes the reins of government. So that, strictly speaking, what the Holy Ghost brings about in the soul when He is honored by the believer is not self-control (i.e., government by self) but divine control (i.e., the government is by Christ).

# OCTOBER 2

*The goat shall bear upon him all their iniquities unto a land not inhabited: and he shall let go the goat in the wilderness.*
—Lev. 16:22

These words, which set before us the type, find their fulfillment in Christ, the antitype. Christ is here presented to us as the Bearer of sin; and in thus bearing sin, putting it away. The high priest laid his hands upon the head of the scapegoat and confessed the sins of the whole nation. Guilt was thus symbolically transferred from Israel, the sinner, to the divinely appointed victim, the substitute. The goat representing Christ thus received the burden of sin. One goat could not set forth all that was comprehended in that divine transaction which atoned for sin on Calvary's cross. Another victim was needed to foreshadow the other side of this important truth. If the scapegoat, which was led out into the wilderness into a land not inhabited, set forth the *result* of Christ's *atoning* death, the sacrifice of the other goat, as an offering for sin to God, represented the meritorious *cause* of this gracious result. He who died for our sins, by that death bore our sins, carried them away, and made an end of them. (See Isa. 53:6, 11, 12; John 1:29; Heb. 9:26.)

# OCTOBER 3

*Unto him that loved us, and washed us from our sins in his own blood.*—Rev. 1:5

The great cause of all our blessings is the love of God. It was a love shown to the unworthy and unclean. What is it that the blood of Christ accomplishes in behalf of every believing soul? First, there is its efficacy Godward. It atones for the guilt of sin. It answers every claim of that righteous law which our transgressions had dishonored and assailed. It removes the condemnation that that law pronounces over every soul that fails either in omission or commission, as touching that law. The blood atones for the sinner, and places him not only in a position of freedom from guilt, but of actual acceptance (Rom. 5:9). Then there is the efficacy of the blood manward. It washes us from sins of defilement. It sets us free from its tyranny. "Unto him that loveth us, and loosed us from our sins by his blood" (ASV). The blood of Christ emancipates us from the bondage and service of sin. If we would know this freedom we must claim by faith that which is already ours by God's gift in Christ.

## OCTOBER 4

*Moses wist not that the skin of his face shone while he talked with him.*—Exod. 34:29

Moses was privileged to go up into the mount and hold intercourse with Jehovah for forty days. What a wonderful conference that must have been! And as God talked with him, the glory of God transfigured the countenance of Moses. But Moses was not occupied with his own shining. He "wist not that the skin of his face shone." He was occupied with "the beauty of holiness" that he beheld in Jehovah Himself. All this typified what the Gospel brings us into today. (See 2 Cor. 3:18.) It is of the first importance that there should be, besides nearness, nothing between the soul and God. How many things there are in our daily life that often do come between! It is not sin only that obstructs the intercourse. It may be care or anxiety. It may be our business, or even the work of the Lord itself. Or we may let some form of Christian experience, which we are seeking to realize, come between our souls and God. Whatever it is it must go, so that there may be *nothing* between our souls and the glory of God.

## OCTOBER 5

*Call upon me in the day of trouble: I will deliver thee, and thou shalt glorify me.*—Ps. 50:15

We have here a *command,* a *promise,* and a *privilege.* The *command* is God's direction as to what we are to do in the day of trouble. "Call upon me." To call upon Him is to throw ourselves upon Him, for strength, or comfort, or deliverance, as the case may be. The day of trouble may be present with us now. If so, it is the very day God has named for you to apply to Him for deliverance. Then there is the *promise*—to encourage our expectation, and to strengthen our faith, God gives us one of His own undertakings. "I will deliver thee." It is for us to pray and trust; it is for Him to fulfill His own promise. We may confidently rely upon Him to do it (1 Thess. 5:24). The *privilege* is one of the greatest that we can possibly enjoy. "Thou shalt glorify me." In ourselves we have neither the power nor the wisdom to do this. But God declares we *shall* glorify Him. By becoming the subjects of His pardoning mercy and renewing grace, we may glorify Him. By being examples of His emancipating power, we may bring glory to His name. (John 15:8; Isa. 61:3; Ps. 50:23.)

# OCTOBER 6

*The Lord God omnipotent reigneth.*—Rev. 19:6

The tried believer has often to remind himself that the God of his salvation is the Lord omnipotent. Without giving way to open unbelief, the soul sometimes yields to the habit of limiting God's grace and power. This was the sin of God's redeemed people of old. "They limited the Holy One of Israel" (Ps. 78:41). That is, they set a limit to His power. They said He could do this, and that, but can He spread a table in the wilderness? This was as much as to say that God was not omnipotent; to deny His omnipotence was to deny His deity. Here then was Israel's sin. Alas! how often God's children are guilty of limiting God! We need ever to keep before us this divine attribute—"The Lord God omnipotent reigneth." He is almighty to save, and to keep. "All power is given unto me in heaven and in earth" (Matt. 28:18). "Some trust in chariots, and some in horses: but we will remember the name of the LORD our God" (Ps. 20:7). That is, we will remember who He is, and what He is. A view of His attributes will calm our fears and deliver us from the sin of unbelief. (See Ps. 9:10; Luke 18:27.)

# OCTOBER 7

*The meek will he teach his way.*—Ps. 25:9

The meek are those who are submissive. They are pliable under the Lord's hand. They are willing to be at the Lord's disposal. They have a teachable spirit. Here is the secret of divine guidance. It is a daily process. He does not reveal the whole plan of His will at once, but gradually, day by day, and step by step. To know His will, and to do it, we must cherish this spirit of meekness. This meekness consists in a spirit of humble dependence upon God, a consciousness of personal weakness and insufficiency, with a restful confidence in God for everything. In that condition of soul we shall have no difficulty about guidance. He will *teach* us His way. That is, He will cause us to know it. There will be no doubt about it. Then He will *guide* us in it. The way to be guided aright, then, is plain. Our first business is to become meek; in others words, to fall at the Master's feet, and to seek from Him this spirit of holy, reverent submission. He will teach us His way of victory, of progress, and of holiness. All our trouble comes from wanting to follow our way.

## OCTOBER 8

*I will not fear what man shall do unto me.*—Heb. 13:6

The inspired writer of this epistle quotes from the Old Testament. "For Himself hath said" is the phrase he uses in making this quotation. The words, in substance, were spoken by Jehovah to Jacob (Gen. 28:15), to Moses (Deut. 31:6, 8), and to Joshua (Josh. 1:5). They were uttered thousands of years before these Christians, to whom this epistle was addressed, came into the world. But the inspired writer has no hesitation in applying them to the children of God in his own day. This teaches us that we need not be afraid to appropriate Old Testament promises because we live in New Testament days (2 Tim. 3:16). And what is it that "He hath said"? "I will in no way fail you, neither will I in any way forsake you." The child of God today may rest with certainty upon that divine assurance. And thus resting, what is it he is privileged to declare? "So that with good courage we say, The Lord is my helper; I will not fear: What shall man do unto me?" (ASV).

## OCTOBER 9

*Thou art a God ready to pardon, gracious and merciful.*
  —Neh. 9:17

God does not need our entreaties to move Him to be gracious to us. He is not a hard, relentless Being, needing our supplications before He will be propitious to us. He waits to be gracious to us. He does not say, "Repent, and then I will have mercy on you." The revelation of his love toward us is antecedent to our faith. Remember "it is the goodness of God" that "leadeth thee to repentance" (Rom. 2:4). It is not the fear of hell, or of future punishment, that brings the soul to contrition. The change of mind, of which true repentance consists, comes from having our false impressions of God removed. It is when we see that, even while we were yet sinners and rebels, God gave His only begotten Son, that melts our hearts. It is a view of His wondrous grace toward us—His attitude of love—that brings us in contrition to His feet. This is the great message of the Gospel which we may proclaim to all men: He is "a God ready to pardon, gracious and merciful." We are called to repentance on the ground of God's gracious and tender mercies toward us (Joel 2:13).

## OCTOBER 10

*The whole family in heaven and earth.*—Eph. 3:15

Or, as it is in the ASV, "from whom every family in heaven and on earth is named." "Every fatherhood," as it is in the margin. The sentence occurs in one of Paul's prayers—one of the most wonderful of the inspired prayers recorded in the Scriptures. In the same epistle the apostle writes, there is "One God and Father of all, who is above all, and through all, and in you all" (Eph. 4:6). There is a sense in which it may be said that God is the Father of all men. But when the apostle speaks of the relation which we are privileged to occupy toward God as Christians, he says of believers only, "Ye are all the children of God by faith in Christ Jesus" (Gal. 3:26). And when he speaks of the Spirit in the same connection, he writes, "For ye have not received the spirit of bondage again to fear; but ye have received the Spirit of adoption, whereby we cry, Abba, Father. The Spirit itself beareth witness with our spirit, that we are the children of God" (Rom. 8:15, 16). Here is the secret of all true and acceptable service. We become God's children before we are called to be His servants.

## OCTOBER 11

*Be not far from me; for trouble is near.*—Ps. 22:11

It is in the hour of trouble that the believer realizes the value and preciousness of the promises of God. God's promises are not intended to dispense with our prayers. It is true God does not need information; nor does He need to be persuaded to be merciful. But He has so ordered it, that if we would know the fulfillment of His promises, we must make our requests known to Him (Phil. 4:6); and so He has said, "He shall call upon me; and I will answer him: I will be with him in trouble; I will deliver him, and honour him" (Ps. 91:15). The presence of the Lord—as a fact revealed to the soul—includes every possible spiritual blessing. "His presence is Salvation."

To cry to God, and to seek His presence, is not to doubt the truth of His promise. It is to plead it. It is like bringing the bank note to the bank to be cashed. As David prayed, "Say unto my soul, I am thy salvation" (Ps. 35:3), so we may ask, "Say unto my soul, 'I am with thee.' Tell me, down in the depths of my heart, that which I know with my head."

# OCTOBER 12

*God was in Christ, reconciling the world unto himself, not imputing their trespasses unto them.*—2 Cor. 5:19

The death of Christ was no mere example of self-sacrifice. It was the divinely appointed method of removing the guilt of sin, and of bringing the sinner to God in peace. It was not an experiment by One who was merely a sinless Man. "But all things" were "of God," who reconciled us to Himself through Christ. God was in Christ. We have no room now for doubt as to whether that work was sufficient or acceptable. Reconciliation on God's side is already effected. His law has been vindicated and His name magnified by that work of atonement. And now the service He commits to His servants here upon earth is called "the ministry of reconciliation." "We are ambassadors therefore on behalf of Christ, as though God were entreating by us; we beseech you on behalf of Christ, be ye reconciled to God" (2 Cor. 5:20, ASV).

To know God in Christ is to know that He is the God of our salvation and to be at peace. Think not that you have to make your peace with Him. That you could never do. Christ has accomplished this through His blood.

# OCTOBER 13

*From the first day that thou didst set thine heart to understand, and to chasten thyself before thy God, thy words were heard.*—Dan. 10:12

Daniel humbled himself before God, not for his own sins only, but for the sins of the whole nation. He was moved with a sense of deep humiliation on account of their sad departure from the God who had so graciously dealt with them. How wonderful that God should have regarded this act on the part of Daniel! But it is only an instance of the truth recorded in Isaiah 57:15, that He is "with him also that is of a contrite and humble spirit." Daniel is a striking example for us of the duty of intercession in behalf, not of individuals only, but in behalf of the whole Church. It is that we may bring down God's blessing on our fellowmen. Let us come to the throne of grace, and not only *pray* on their behalf, but *chasten ourselves* before God, by sincere confession and humiliation for the sins of our day and generation. "From the first day that thou didst set thine heart" to do this, saith the Lord, "thy words were heard." What assurance of answered prayer!

## OCTOBER 14

*Christ both died, and rose, and revived, that he might be Lord both of the dead and living.*—Rom. 14:9

"That he might be Lord." What thought could be more gladdening to the believer than this?—that He, who has revealed Himself to the soul as "Jesus"—the One who died and shed His blood for us, and who has also manifested Himself as the "Christ"—the anointed One, and the One from whom we receive "the anointing"—should still further unveil Himself to the soul as the "Lord." It was for this that "Christ both died and lived again."

What is it to know Him within us as "Lord"? It is something more than a knowledge of His justifying grace, more than a knowledge of His intercession within the veil. When He is "Lord" in the heart of the believer, divine power controls the being—a power that transforms the inner experience, as well as the outward conduct. It was in this way the Apostle Paul preached Christ. "We preach not ourselves, but Christ Jesus the *Lord*" (2 Cor. 4:5).

## OCTOBER 15

*God is my defence.*—Ps. 59:9

The strength of the believer against his foes does not consist in what he is in himself, but in what God is for him. The believer, however, must avail himself of that strength; he must appropriate, by faith, what God is for him. When he can say, "God is my defence," it implies that he has forsaken all false confidences, and has retreated into his castle. "The name of the LORD is a strong tower" (Prov. 18:10). But how am I to have the benefit of the strength of that tower? By "running into it." When the little child has the walls of an impregnable fort between himself and the enemy, he is as strong as the full-grown man who is within the same fortress. His strength is not a question of growth or attainment, but of position. His safety and defense is not in himself, but in the fortress. So it is with the believer. It is a question of relationship to Christ. Where do I stand? What is the ground that I occupy? Where do I live spiritually? "The LORD is my rock, and my fortress . . . in him will I trust" (2 Sam. 22:2, 3). The great lesson of life, when we have found our Refuge, is to know how to *abide* in Him. (See Ps. 28:7; Isa. 59:19; Heb. 13:6.)

# OCTOBER 16

*Not slothful in business; fervent in spirit; serving the Lord.*
   —Rom. 12:11

"The precept *includes* an exhortation to thoroughness in earthly duty, but much more besides" *(Bishop Moule)*. The context refers to the "acts of human thought and energy," and "favours the reference to *man's* spirit renewed and animated by grace" *(Bishop Moule)*. The words suggest that there is a danger of indolence in relation to the duties of life, and enforce the necessity of activity and diligence in everything that we are called upon to do. We notice here how the responsibilities in the two spheres of life, the earthly and the heavenly, are linked together. Instances of this precept we find in the following Old Testament saints—Noah: "Thee have I seen righteous before me in this generation" (Gen. 7:1). Abraham: "I know him, that he will command his children and his household after him, . . . to do justice and judgment" (Gen. 18:19). Joshua: "As for me and my house, we will serve the LORD" (Josh. 24:14, 15). Josiah (2 Chron. 34:3, 31, 33). The secret is found in being filled with the Holy Ghost.

# OCTOBER 17

*In thy name shall they rejoice all the day; and in thy right-eousness shall they be exalted.*—Ps. 89:16

To rejoice in God's name is to find our consolation and strength in the Lord Himself, in His attributes and perfections. It is to see that God is for us. All that God is, His wisdom, and goodness, and power, and holiness, and truth, and love, are engaged to make the believer blessed. This is the ground of our joy. And inasmuch as God is the same yesterday and today and for ever, we may rejoice "all the day." Circumstances may change, trial and sorrow may overtake us, but God will remain ever the same; and so we may continue to rejoice.

Then, under God's righteous government, His people are lifted up above the power of their enemies. They find salvation and honor, and hereafter they will be exalted to heavenly glory and dignity. "To him that overcometh will I grant to sit with me in my throne" (Rev. 3:21). But in another sense the righteousness of God is the secret of the believer's exaltation, because it places him above the power of the law to condemn. He is in that righteousness exalted to a position of complete acceptance.

## OCTOBER 18

*One of the soldiers with a spear pierced his side, and forth-*
*with came there out blood and water.—John 19:34*

"The wantonness of the soldiers' violence was in part
checked ('They brake not His legs'); but one of them, in
order no doubt to learn the certainty of the Lord's death,
'pierced His side.' The word which describes the wound
is used both of a light touch and of a deep gash. Here
there is no doubt that the latter is described, both from
the weapon used (the long lance of a horseman) and from
the object of the blow" *(Bishop Westcott)*. The reality of
Christ's death is thus clearly attested. John, who records
the incident, seems to be impressed with the miraculous
character of that which immediately followed His death.
This is evident from the words, "And he that saw it bare
record, and his record is true: and he knoweth that he
saith true, that ye might believe."

"In the water and the blood are represented the most
essential blessings of salvation: the *water* chiefly symbolizes
the moral purifying power of the work of Christ; the *blood*
points out the ransom paid for our guilt, as well as the atoning sacrifice *(Krummacher)*.

## OCTOBER 19

*The* LORD *shall be thy confidence, and shall keep thy foot from*
*being taken.—Prov. 3:26*

Confidence means reliance. To rely on anything, or any
one, is to depend or lean upon that person or thing, with
the assurance that we have something there that is trust-
worthy. Confidence in something is natural to every man.
Now when that confidence is *in the Lord,* the man passes
from the natural to the spiritual. Confidence in the Lord
means *repose* in Him. This is the secret of composure—
and composure is the secret of power. The Lord "shall
keep thy foot from being taken." This implies that we walk
in the midst of danger. The enemy of souls sets many a
trap to catch the feet of God's children. But the Lord
"will keep the feet of his saints" (1 Sam. 2:9). "The steps
of a good man are ordered by the LORD: and he delighteth in his way" (Ps. 37:23). But how does the Lord keep
the feet of His people? Not by dealing with them as if they
were mere machines. He keeps us by giving us the grace
of holy vigilance; by teaching us ever to be looking to
Him; not to watch the enemy so much as the Lord, who
is our Confidence.

## OCTOBER 20

*I delight in the law of God after the inward man.*—Rom. 7:22

These words are the language of a renewed heart. None but those who have been quickened by the Spirit could give utterance to such a sentiment. It implies a sympathetic relation between his inmost being and the divine law. "I rejoice *with* the law of God." It indicates an inward harmony with God's will and commandments. If there were no other reasons, this one alone would be sufficient to show that the seventh chapter of Romans is not the experience of an unconverted man. It is the language throughout of a Christian. But it must not be isolated from the context. The opening words of the eighth chapter must be taken in close connection with what he declares in the seventh. "The law of sin" in our members cannot be destroyed or suspended, but it may be effectually counteracted, so that practically and experimentally we may be *made free* from it. This is brought about by the influence of another law—"the law of the Spirit of life in Christ Jesus" (Rom. 8:2). Here is an opposing law to the law of sin, superior to it, and perpetually in force, as long as we are abiding in Christ—"in Christ Jesus."

## OCTOBER 21

*[Out of] his fulness have all we received, and grace for grace.*
—John 1:16

Christ is "full of grace and truth" (John 1:14). Who can estimate the extent of the spiritual wealth we have in Him? "As applied to the Lord, the phrase ('full of grace and truth') marks Him as the Author of perfect Redemption and perfect Revelation. Grace corresponds with the idea of the revelation of God as love (1 John 4:8, 16), by Him who is life and truth; with that of the revelation of God as light (1 John 1:5), by Him who is Himself light" *(Bishop Westcott).* Out of His fullness, as a copious source of blessing, have all we received—he is speaking of believers—that which answers to our wants. "And grace for grace." That is, grace *instead* of grace. Each blessing appropriated becomes the foundation of a greater blessing. Today's grace takes the place of yesterday's grace. There is a constant stream of grace that brings about a perpetually recurring exchange of "grace for grace." This teaches us that there is no such thing as stagnation in a healthy spiritual life and that the supplies which meet our present needs are also intended to increase our capacities for further gifts.

# OCTOBER 22

*O God, my heart is fixed.*—Ps. 108:1

What is a fixed heart? It is not a heart that is full of confidence or of faith merely, but a heart whose faith is centered on God. It is not faith that is the secret of the heart's fixedness, but the Rock Christ Jesus, on whom faith reposes its confidence. There is only one Center that is absolutely immovable and unchangeable. And that is God. The strength or stability of the believer is not due to the tenacity of his grasp, so much as to the firmness of the Rock on which he rests. We must not look at our faith, but at Him on whom our faith depends. This condition of rest being reached, all fear vanishes. "The LORD is my light and my salvation; whom shall I fear? the LORD is the strength of my life; of whom shall I be afraid?" (Ps. 27:1).

A fixed heart is a praising heart. "I will sing and give praise, even with my glory" (Ps. 108:1). By his "glory" the poet means his soul, and all the capacities and faculties which belonged to him as an intelligent being, created in the divine image.

# OCTOBER 23

*A man's life consisteth not in the abundance of the things which he possesseth.*—Luke 12:15

We often fancy that a true life means a successful life, in the sense of outward prosperity. But this is not our Lord's conception of life; He gives us a striking contrast in the case of Dives and Lazarus which teaches us quite the opposite truth (Luke 16:19). Another example to the same end we have in the case of the rich ruler (Luke 18:18). What is a man's life, according to the divine standard? What should it consist in? In being consecrated to the will of God. The really successful life is that life which is simply following the path that God has marked out for it. God has created our life in Christ Jesus unto good works (Eph. 2:10). He has exactly fitted it to the end to which He has called it. He marks out its course, He prepares the good works for it to engage in, and He energizes it with all the strength needed to fulfill its end. It is not in the abundance of the things we possess that life consists. These are mere outside appendages, and form no essential part of our life. The life that brings glory to God is the life that also brings blessing to mankind.

# OCTOBER 24

*I am cast out of thy sight; yet I will look again toward thy holy temple.*—Jonah 2:4

A wrong idea of God is a serious hindrance to prayer. Jonah, though he was not ignorant of God's existence and believed in His power, needed to learn much touching His love and His grace. The end of all God's dealings with us is to bring us to Himself; to bring us to Him in prayer; to teach us to approach Him with a true spirit of filial confidence. Though we have a saving knowledge of God, there may yet be much misconception as to His true character. Often we may fall into error by thinking of Him as less loving, less merciful and gracious, than He is. We may look at Him through the medium of adverse circumstances and interpret Him by what we see and feel. This is not the way of faith. Then it is we are tempted to say, "I am cast out of thy sight." But when we regard Him by the way of faith, then we learn to interpret circumstances by what God is, as He has revealed Himself to us through His Word, and in His Son Jesus Christ. Here we have the secret of liberty and power in prayer.

# OCTOBER 25

*Lo, I am with you alway, even unto the end of the world.*—Matt. 28:20

As a well-known preacher has said, "It was a strange fact that He should, for the first time, promise to be with them always, at the very last moment before vanishing from the world; and we may be certain that words apparently so contradictory have a very deep significance. ... The meaning of this saying ('Lo, I am with you alway') was, that His departure would really be the commencement of His nearer presence as a Friend than they had known while they saw Him with the bodily eye."

That presence is a special presence. God is everywhere. But the Lord speaks now of His special presence with His people. It is a spiritual presence. Jesus—the visible human but glorified nature—is in heaven. But Christ, the spiritual risen Lord of life and glory—He is in and with His Church on earth, as well as on the throne in heaven.

It is a sanctifying presence. Holiness has its embodiment in Him. We are holy as we are in Him and He in us. Spiritual and moral transfiguration is the result of being brought into union and fellowship with the Holy One.

# OCTOBER 26

*The* LORD *reigneth.*—Ps. 99:1

It is especially in the midst of His Church that the Lord's throne is established. Though to Him all authority has been given in heaven and in earth, the earth is not yet the sphere in which His sovereignty is recognized or His will obeyed. Still, all things are under His hand. All powers and forces are at His command. Not a single event or circumstance of life can happen without His knowledge and permission. This is a fact of unspeakable comfort to the believer, when sin seems to be triumphant and darkness covers the earth. It is because the Lord is omnipotent, and holds the reins of government, that the psalmist could say, "Let the earth rejoice; let the multitude of isles be glad thereof." The believer looks through all second causes. He remembers the words of the prophet, and realizes their truth today—"He changeth the times and the seasons; he removeth kings, and setteth up kings; he giveth wisdom unto the wise, and knowledge to them that know understanding" (Dan. 2:21). Jesus said, "All power is given unto me in heaven and in earth" (Matt. 28:18).

# OCTOBER 27

*Himself took our infirmities, and bare our sicknesses.*—Matt. 8:17

The fact here recorded shows us the perfection of Christ's sympathy. He is "touched with the feeling of our infirmities" (Heb. 4:15). Though He had no sin, yet He knew by actual experience that which was the consequence of sin, namely, suffering. He knew what pain was, arising from hunger and fatigue. All this shows us the completeness of Christ's identity with us in our humanity. Identity is the secret of all true sympathy.

The words are a prophecy of better days for the redeemed. They are an evidence that disease does not belong to the true order of nature.

But in Christ we see not only a perfect Man full of sympathy, but a supreme Lord full of power. "And Jesus, moved with compassion, put forth his hand, and touched him, and saith unto him, I will; be thou clean. And as soon as he had spoken, . . . the leprosy departed from him, and he was cleansed" (Mark 1:41, 42). Man needs something more than pity to sympathize with him; he needs power sufficient to deliver him out of his misery (Isa. 53:6).

## OCTOBER 28

*He saw that there was no man, and wondered that there was no intercessor; therefore his arm brought salvation unto him.*—Isa. 59:16

Here we see both the Father and the Son in connection with our salvation. There was no one who was ready or able to come to the rescue. There was none to stay the plague like Moses and Aaron (Num. 16:47, 48), or Phinehas (Num. 25:7); therefore His own arm wrought salvation for Him (Ps. 98:1). In Isaiah 53:1 Christ is spoken of as "the arm of the Lord," and in the 12th verse of that chapter He is seen as making intercession. God's arm brought salvation to Him. The figure is beautiful and suggestive. How it speaks of power and skill, as well as of nearness to Him who stretches it out in mercy and love! Salvation is spoken of here as something brought to God, not simply as something held out to men. This shows how His heart is bound up in it, how He delights in it. He calls it His salvation, not only because He has provided it, but because it belongs to Him, and He takes infinite interest in all who are brought within its range. We see then how truly "salvation is of the Lord." God Himself is its source and power.

## OCTOBER 29

*He is altogether lovely.*—Song of Solomon 5:16

When Christ manifests Himself to the believer as He does not to the world, His surpassing attractiveness fills the soul with rapture. The joy that gladdens his heart is not a senseless emotion. It is an intelligent delight, because it is founded on the fact that Christ's perfections exactly meet the deep necessities of our being. The words imply that the soul of the believer has made some progress in the spiritual life. It is not alone with doctrines, or truth in the abstract, that he is concerned, but with a living Person. Truth may meet the cravings of our understandings, but it is only the personal Savior who can satisfy the longings of our hearts. We have not only to know and believe that salvation is provided. We have to be drawn to Him who is altogether lovely. "Whom having not seen, ye love" (1 Peter 1:8). We not only believe in His Word, and rely on His all-sufficiency and faithfulness; we may so know Him that our hearts shall burn within us with deepest affection toward Him. Love, like faith, does not come by looking in upon ourselves, but by gazing upon Him.

# OCTOBER 30

*It is good that a man should both hope and quietly wait for the salvation of the LORD.*—Lam. 3:26

What is "the salvation of the LORD"? It is something more than the blessing that comes to the sinner when, on his first coming to Christ, he passes from death to life. It is the deliverance that he needs amid all the temptations and trials that meet him in his journey heavenward. He has come to Christ. He has found life, and pardon, and peace through "the blood of his cross," but he still needs a daily salvation from sinning. The only salvation worth anything, either for standing or walking—for life or for godliness—is the "salvation of the LORD." Now, it is here said that it is good that a man should "hope" for that salvation. This may be said to be the first condition of enjoying. "Hope" implies both desire and expectation. A person may desire a blessing without expecting to receive it. He may desire it intensely, and yet have no real faith that it is possible for him to have it. Such a soul can make no progress. He will not, as long as he continues in that attitude, be brought to know what "the fullness of blessing" means in the daily life.

# OCTOBER 31

*Not by might, nor by power, but by my Spirit, saith the LORD of hosts.*—Zech. 4:6

God's victories are not achieved by human energy or natural strength. They are wrought by a spiritual force. Not by an abstract power, but by a personal Spirit. "My Spirit, saith the LORD of hosts." God is speaking, not of a mere influence or emanation, but of the third Person of the blessed Trinity—the Holy Ghost. He is set forth in this chapter under a beautiful and striking emblem. The golden oil that flowed from the golden bowl, through the golden pipes, was the secret of the brightness and illuminating power of the golden candlestick. So the Holy Spirit is the believer's secret of success in all work for God. He is the "unction"—the anointing that comes to us from the "Holy One" (1 John 2:20). How often do we forget where our true strength lies! How often have we laboriously struggled and put forth every energy to accomplish our work! And how miserably we have failed, because we have not honored God the Holy Ghost!

# NOVEMBER 1

*Blessed is the man that heareth me, watching daily at my gates, waiting at the posts of my doors.*—Prov. 8:34

The two prominent thoughts here are the Person and the means of grace that He appoints. "That heareth me." Faith arises so truly above the things of sense that the Lord is recognized as speaking even now. It is not the mere letter of the Scripture that we listen to, but to the divine voice in that letter. The Lord is ever speaking to us. "I will hear what God the Lord will speak." "Blessed" is that man who is willing to hear God's voice, because to be willing to hear means being ready to do what He calls us to do.

But this hearkening to His voice is not something so superhuman that the ordinary means of grace are despised or neglected. It is essentially practical. It is only as we watch daily at His gates, and wait at the posts of His doors, that we hear His voice. The grace that makes this hearkening a reality has transformed the empty forms into overflowing channels of divine quickening. "This shall be a continual burnt offering throughout your generations." (See Ex. 29:42.)

# NOVEMBER 2

*Ever follow that which is good.*—1 Thess. 5:15

The term "good" to the believer is suggestive of many thoughts. It of course means "good" in the abstract— "Whatsoever things are true, whatsoever things are honest, whatsoever things are just, whatsoever things are pure, whatsoever things are lovely, whatsoever things are of good report" (Phil. 4:8). But to the believer everything that is good is but a ray that comes forth from the One center—the Good One. "Why callest thou me good?" said our Lord to the young man in the gospel (Matt. 19:17). "There is none good but . . . God."

The questioner had lightly applied the word "good" to One whom he as yet regarded only as a human teacher. What he needed, therefore, was to be brought to such a view of Christ as to see that all goodness in its absolute and infinite sense found its embodiment in Him. So with the believer today. He has to see that goodness in the abstract is not sufficient either as a pattern or as a power, for his spiritual transformation and practical walk. To "follow that which is good" means to him to follow the good One.

## NOVEMBER 3

*The ways of the* Lord *are right, and the just shall walk in them: but the transgressors shall fall therein.*—Hos. 14:9

It has been well said, "There is enough of saving truth clear in God's Word to guide those humbly seeking salvation, and enough of difficulties to confound those who curiously seek them out, rather than practically seek salvation." How true it is that what God's Word is to us depends very much upon the spirit in which we come to it, and our motive in reading it. The "just" in this passage are the righteous—and the righteous are those who in Christ are "justified." To such God's ways are right. They commend themselves to the heart and the head of the believer. God's ways are something beyond His works. Many see His works who do not know His ways. "He made known his ways unto Moses, his acts unto the children of Israel" (Ps. 103:7). There is no greater privilege than to walk in the ways of the Lord. We may see them and admire them, and yet not walk in them. To walk in them is to find that His "ways are ways of pleasantness," and all His "paths are peace" (Prov. 3:17).

## NOVEMBER 4

*Now for a season, if need be, ye are in heaviness through manifold temptations.*—1 Pet. 1:6

Literally, the meaning is, "After having been grieved in the present (if it must be so) for a little while, in the midst of manifold temptations." What these temptations were we are not told. But it was a trial, it would seem, that brought all Christians alike under the same suffering. It arose, no doubt, from the hostile attitude of the Gentile neighbors (*see* ch. 2:12, 15; 3:14-17; 4:4, 12-19). These Hebrew Christians, it would seem, felt what many young Christians have felt in the present day, that this persecution and suffering was not what was to be expected. They seemed to think that it was not what the Scriptures promised, that to attach themselves to the Messiah was to have a life of sorrow in the world. But the apostle would show them how that in the midst of the suffering there might be joy unspeakable and full of glory (1 Pet. 1:8). He exhorts them not to regard these things as strange. They are included in the purposes of God, and have been amply provided for by Him. We need not, therefore, be cast down or discouraged.

# NOVEMBER 5

*Take thou also unto thee principal spices ... and thou shalt make it an oil of holy ointment.*—Exod. 30:23, 25

The anointing oil would seem to be the type of the Holy Spirit; of that Spirit that rested on the Lord Jesus. "The spirit of the LORD shall rest upon him; the spirit of wisdom and understanding, the spirit of counsel and might, the spirit of knowledge and of the fear of the LORD; and shall make him of quick understanding in the fear of the LORD" (Isa. 11:2, 3). It is worthy of notice that the way in which these graces of the Spirit are arranged in Isaiah has some analogy to the proportions of the spices in the anointing oil *(Soltau)*. "The holy oil had infused into it the essence of four 'principal spices'—myrrh, that scents the garments of the great king (Ps. 45:8; S. of Sol. 3:6); cinnamon, the choicest of the spices of distant India; sweet calamus, that exhales its best fragrance when bruised; cassia, which, together with sweet calamus, formed one of the glories of the market of Tyre" (Ezek. 27:19).

# NOVEMBER 6

*When Christ, who is our life, shall appear, then shall ye also appear with him in glory.*—Col. 3:4

Christ shall be manifested. That is, He shall leave the "secret place of His glory and return to human sight, in His second advent." He shall be manifested not to our bodily eye merely, but to our mental and spiritual vision also, in such a way that we shall see Him "as he is." That vision of Christ will have a transforming effect upon every child of God. Our bodies as well as our spiritual beings will be transfigured into the likeness of His glory. We shall also appear with Him in glory. The oneness of the members with the Head "will be seen, in all its living power and wonder, and their perfect holiness will be discovered to be all of Him." He is our "Life"—the life that is hid in Him. "The Holy Spirit is 'the Lord, the Life-Giver' (Nicene Creed); but *the Life* is the Son of God, as the Redeemer and Head of His saints" *(Bishop Moule)*. Compare John 6:57; 11:25; 14:6; Gal. 2:20; 1 John 5:11, 12. Though at present that life is "hidden," still it is the power that now worketh in us. The believer must do all in the energy of that life—Christ in Him.

## NOVEMBER 7

*Oh that men would praise the* LORD *for his goodness, and for his wonderful works to the children of men.*—Ps. 107:8

It is praise which, in a special sense, glorifies God. "Whoso offereth praise glorifieth me" (Ps. 50:23). But men do not praise God until they have hearts to know the "goodness" of the Lord. There must be personal and experimental knowledge of that goodness. "O taste and see that the LORD is good: blessed is the man that trusteth in him" (Ps. 34:8). It is a view of what He has done for us as sinners that awakens our gratitude and kindles within us the song of praise. Praise is what God looks for from those whom He has redeemed—"This people have I formed for myself; they shall shew forth my praise" (Isa. 43:21). "That we should be to the praise of his glory" (Eph. 1:12).

Let this thought search our hearts. "Am I living a life that is to the praise of God's glory?" The charge that God brings home to Belshazzar through the prophet Daniel is this: "The God in whose hand thy breath is, and whose are all thy ways, hast thou not glorified" (Dan 5:23).

## NOVEMBER 8

*Let us, who are of the day, be sober, putting on the breastplate of faith and love; and for an helmet, the hope of salvation.*—1 Thess. 5:8

There is a danger lest those "who are of the day" should conform in habit and life with those "who are of the night." It is possible for quickened souls to sleep as do others—nay, to become identified with those who are dead. It is to the children of God who have thus relapsed that those words are addressed. "Awake, thou that sleepest, and arise from among the dead, and Christ shall give thee light." Life they have already, but they have fallen back into the darkness. Drowsiness has overtaken them, and they are overcome by sleep. They are asleep among the dead. They are called to "awake" and to "arise." We have to hear that voice and obey the summons. We have to "stand therefore, having your loins girt about with truth, and having on the breastplate of righteousness ... above all, taking the shield of faith, wherewith ye shall be able to quench all the fiery darts of the wicked" (Eph. 6:14-16). It is only thus equipped that we shall be ready for the conflict or prepared for the sudden assaults of the enemy.

## NOVEMBER 9

*I have laid help upon one that is mighty; I have exalted one chosen out of the people.*—Ps. 89:19

Hengstenberg translates, "I have laid help upon a man of war." And Alexander says that the word "chosen" has "allusion to its specific use as signifying a young warrior." David was elected of God as the champion of Israel to lead her armies to battle and to victory. At the beginning of his career the people cried, "Saul hath slain his thousands, and David his ten thousands." And at the close of his career Israel was victorious over all her enemies, and was at peace. So the Lord Jesus Christ is God's elect to save the souls of men. He is "mighty to save." It is upon Him, the mighty One, that our help is laid. "He is able also to save them to the uttermost that come unto God by him." "Behold my servant, whom I uphold; mine elect, in whom my soul delighteth" (Isa. 42:1).

Because Jesus was "chosen out of the people," He possesses that sympathy with us needed to render His help efficient, and to assure us that it will be imparted. He is "touched with the feeling of our infirmities" (Heb. 4:15).

## NOVEMBER 10

*Fruitful in every good work, and increasing in the knowledge of God.*—Col. 1:10

To be fruitful in the sense of engaging in "every good work" is one thing, and to be fruitful *in* every good work that we are engaged in is another. In the first sense the *multiplicity* of good works is the thought before us—in the other, the *fruitfulness* of our lives is the thing emphasized. You may be busy in a number of good works, and *fruitful* in none of them. You may be perpetually giving way to irritability, to anxious worry, to pride, to harsh judgments and evil-speaking. Well, however active and busy you may be in all these good works, you will not be "fruitful" in them. Fruit is not the outcome of outward action, but of the inner life. Fruit is the result of the Holy Spirit's indwelling—of His gracious, unhindered activity within us. It is not the result of human energy, nor is it the product of the Spirit's power apart from the cooperation of our wills and affections. We yield ourselves to Him, and He takes full possession of our whole beings, and brings every power and faculty of our renewed nature into contribution to this end, that we should bear much fruit.

## NOVEMBER 11

*He led them on safely.*—Ps. 78:53

Before we are ready to consider the "way," we must be sure as to the destination. "Where am I going?" That is the first question. Then comes the inquiry as to the road we are pursuing. The destination is not a place merely, but a Person. "He died the just for the unjust, that He might *bring us to God*" (1 Pet. 3:18). The right way is the way that leads to God. He brings us now into God's presence. We have access through Him into the Holiest. And He will hereafter present us "faultless before the presence of his glory with exceeding joy" (Jude 24). "He led them forth by the right way, that they might go to a city of habitation" (Ps. 107:7).

The perpetual presence of Christ as the Guide of His people is a great and blessed reality. "HE led them." Though pardoned and redeemed, quickened and set free, they are not able to guide themselves. They are as helpless in the journey as they were in the "horrible pit." "HE brought me up also out of an horrible pit, out of the miry clay, and set my feet upon a rock, and established my goings." *"Thou* hast delivered my soul from death: wilt not *thou* deliver my feet from falling?" (Ps. 56:13).

## NOVEMBER 12

*Godly sorrow worketh repentance . . . not to be repented of.* —2 Cor. 7:10

The sorrow which is according to God is very different from other sorrow. It is different in its nature as well as in its effects. When a man sees his sins in connection with God's glory, he realizes their true character. He sees the sinfulness of sin. He sees that it is something which God hates. He learns also to loathe his sins. He is troubled and distressed because of them. This is godly sorrow. He is more concerned on account of the abominable nature of sin, than of the misery which sin brings with it. This is a sorrow that works repentance. That is a change of mind. True repentance is a change of mind toward God. It is something more than mere regret, or even contrition. It is a change of mind. Man's mind is all wrong touching God's character. The Gospel is a revelation of the goodness of God toward man as a sinner. When that goodness is seen and believed in, man's mind is changed toward God. It is the goodness of God that leads us to repentance (Rom. 2:4). Accompanying that change of mind there is sorrow and contrition.

## NOVEMBER 13

*Christ also loved the church, and gave himself for it; that he might sanctify and cleanse it with the washing of water by the word.*—Eph. 5:25, 26

That which moved Him to sacrifice Himself for us was His own sovereign love toward us. He "loved me, and gave himself for me" (Gal. 2:20). And one object of that sacrifice for the Church was this, that He might sanctify it. This must not be understood as meaning that He might *purify* it—though of course this was also the purpose of His death. To "sanctify," in the New Testament, is not synonymous with to "purify." Christ said, "I sanctify myself"; but He could not have said, "I purify myself." To purify implies previous impurity. To sanctify is to consecrate to God. It is to make holy—to set apart unto the Holy One, and thus to make holy. The Revised Standard Version throws light on the passage. "That he might sanctify her, having cleansed her by the washing of water with the word." The dedication of the Church to God follows the cleansing. This special purpose of Christ's death should be often in our thoughts. It will teach us to see not merely what we are saved *from,* but what we have been saved *unto* (Tit. 2:14).

## NOVEMBER 14

*Thou art my help and my deliverer; make no tarrying, O my God.*—Ps. 40:17

These words may be read as the language of David, of Christ, and of the Church. We need not hesitate to apply this Psalm to the Messiah, since we read in Hebrews 10:5-9, the verses 6 to 9 are thus interpreted. The verse that immediately precedes our text is very beautiful, and exactly expresses the feelings of the troubled soul—"As for me I am poor and needy, but the Lord thinks of me" *(Dr. Kay).* Whatever I am in the way of weakness and need God is to me in the way of power and supply. Circumstances of trial and distress are often necessary to give us an experimental knowledge of what God can be to us. A weak faith may pray, *"Be Thou* my Help and my Deliverer"; but it is triumphant faith that says, *"Thou art."* "Thou art my hiding place; thou shalt preserve me from trouble; thou shalt compass me about with songs of deliverance" (Ps. 32:7). The promise pleaded in faith becomes the fact realized in experience. "I am with thee to deliver thee" is the divine answer. "Thou art my deliverer" is faith's answer.

## NOVEMBER 15

*God is faithful, by whom ye were called unto the fellowship of his Son Jesus Christ our Lord.*—1 Cor. 1:9

Some passages of Scripture declare to us what we have been called "out of"; this verse shows us what we have been called "unto." It is "unto the fellowship of his Son Jesus Christ our Lord." By the term "fellowship" we are to understand "something inward and present" *(Godet)*. He is not here speaking of the glorified state in heaven, but of spiritual privilege here on earth. The apostle is speaking of our present participation in Christ's life, the intimate union that subsists between the believer and the Son of God. All that Christ is as the Redeemer—wisdom, righteousness, sanctification, and redemption—the believer partakes in. The call of God in connection with His faithfulness occurs in another passage: "Faithful is he that calleth you, who also will do it" (1 Thess. 5:24).

God's faithfulness is the thought that is so strengthening to faith, as we consider all His wondrous undertakings. Our growth in grace, our conformity to Christ—all depend upon the fulfillment of God's gracious promises.

## NOVEMBER 16

*Sanctify them through thy truth: thy word is truth.*—John 17:17

Christ is our Sanctification. The Holy Spirit is our Sanctifier. And the truth, or word of God, is the instrument the Holy Spirit uses in sanctifying us. We are sanctified by the truth in proportion as the powers and faculties of our being are brought under the sway of that truth. There are forces and qualities of our nature that may be used either for good or evil, such as reason, imagination, prudence, endurance, courage. Now the truth sanctifies us when it appropriates these qualities, and consecrates them to the service of God. The truth is called the "engrafted word" (Jas. 1:21), because just as a graft appropriates the life of the tree, and brings it into contribution to itself, so the word which has found an entrance into our inmost being has the power of drawing out all that is excellent in the natural character, and transforming it into Christian virtue. The wild rose on the bramble becomes the beautifully developed and fragrant flower on the graft; so these moral qualities, which may exist in a pagan, become transfigured by the engrafted word, and the life of the indwelling Holy Ghost.

# NOVEMBER 17

*Thy thoughts are very deep.*—Ps. 92:5

David often refers to God's thoughts. In another Psalm he says, "How precious also are thy thoughts unto me, O God! how great is the sum of them!" (Ps. 139:17). Here he dwells upon the fact of their exceeding depth. God's purposes, plans, and designs are beyond man's power of comprehension—they are past his finding out. But though they are beyond our power of research, we are not left in ignorance of them, because He reveals them unto us in His Word and by His Spirit. "O the depth of the riches both of the wisdom and knowledge of God! how unsearchable are his judgments, and his ways past finding out" (Rom. 11:33). One reason why the Gospel of Christ is misunderstood by some and rejected by others is because God's mode of dealing with sinners is so different from man's method. "My thoughts are not your thoughts, neither are your ways my ways, saith the LORD. For as the heavens are higher than the earth, so are my ways higher than your ways, and my thoughts than your thoughts" (Isa. 55:8, 9).

# NOVEMBER 18

*He stayeth his rough wind in the day of the east wind.*—Isa. 27:8

These words show us how God moderates His chastisements in the day of His judgments. There is nothing hasty, rash, or inconsiderate in His doings. God's chastisements have for their end the recovery of those whom He chastens, and would not be effectual for this end unless they were carefully apportioned and adjusted to the particular case. Thus measure is needed in chastisements. Those which inflict are measured with marvelous exactitude. "In measure he contends with them." David felt this when recognizing that he deserved punishment, he said, "Let us fall now into the hand of the LORD; for his mercies are great" (2 Sam 24:14), "I am with thee, saith the LORD, to save thee . . . I will correct thee in measure, and will not leave thee altogether unpunished" (Jer. 30:11). "For he knoweth our frame; he remembereth that we are dust" (Ps. 103:14). How comforting too is the truth contained in these words: "God is faithful, who will not suffer you to be tempted above that ye are able; but will with the temptation also make a way to escape, that ye may be able to bear it" (1 Cor. 10:13).

## NOVEMBER 19

*By their fruits ye shall know them.*—Matt. 7:20

There are three things in the Christian life that should be distinguished—fruit, gifts, and works. A man may be busy in Christian work without abounding in fruit. Fruit is something higher and more spiritual than works. It is the outcome of the divine life in the soul. The fruit of the Spirit is absent in the life of the man who is habitually grieving the Holy Ghost, however active in work and zealous in doctrine he may be. We have to be *fruitful in every good work*. It is not by their *works* ye shall know them, but by their *fruits*.

Then, again, let us remember that fruit and gifts are not to be confounded. A man may be gifted as a preacher or teacher of the Word, who is nevertheless lacking in the fruit of the Spirit. Those "gifts" may draw crowds, and hundreds may be brought to Christ through the Word preached, and yet if we judged of the man's true spiritual condition by his "gifts," we should come to a wrong conclusion. "By their *fruits* ye shall know them." Let there be genuine humility, an ignoring of self, and you have then "fruit," which is distinct from "works" and from "gifts."

## NOVEMBER 20

*When I sit in darkness, the* Lord *shall be a light unto me.*
—Micah 7:8

We must read the whole verse to take in the meaning of these words: "Rejoice not against me, O mine enemy: when I fall, I shall arise." That is the sentence that precedes, and the words that follow our text are: "I will bear the indignation of the Lord, because I have sinned against him." It is the language we see of a child of God who has sinned—grievously sinned it may be. God's righteous indignation is recognized as that which the soul deserves. Sitting in darkness is the condition which is the just consequences of transgression. The world looks on in exultation. It rejoices over the falls of the children of God. It would persuade them there was no hope of forgiveness. But the language of faith is, "When I fall, I shall arise; when I sit in darkness, the Lord shall be a light unto me." It is good for the backsliding believer to remember this.

How often when men sin they think relief is to be sought from time; that the guilt is put away when it is forgotten by the transgressor himself. Or they fancy that amendment is an expiation.

## NOVEMBER 21

*Him that cometh to me I will in no wise cast out.*—John 6:37

Looking at the whole passaage, we notice that our LORD gives us here two sides of the same truth—the divine and the human side. "All that the Father giveth me shall come to me," and "him that cometh to me I will in no wise cast out." Dr. David Brown puts it thus: "As the former was the *Divine,* this is just the *human* side of the same thing. True the 'coming' ones of the second clause are just the 'given' ones of the first. But had our Lord merely said, *'When those that have been given Me of My Father shall come to Me, I will receive them'*—besides being very flat, the impression conveyed would have been quite different, sounding as if there were *no other laws in operation,* in the movement of sinners towards Christ, but such as are wholly *Divine* and *inscrutable* to us; whereas, though He does speak of it as a sublime certainty, which men's *refusals* cannot frustrate, He speaks of that certainty as taking effect only by men's *voluntary advances* to Him and acceptance of Him—'Him that cometh to Me,' 'Whosoever will.' Only it is not simply *willing,* but *coming."*

## NOVEMBER 22

*Praying in the Holy Ghost.*—Jude 20

There are three things insisted upon in this passage as the means by which the main exhortation is to be obeyed. That exhortation we have in the words, "Keep yourselves in the love of God." Recognize the fact that that love has already been revealed. It is not something we have to awaken, or originate by some action of our own. When our eyes are opened we discover that it already exists. God's love is one of the first great facts of divine revelation which we have to behold and appropriate. As believers in Jesus Christ it is our privilege to know that it has not only been shown toward us, it is the very atmosphere into which we have been introduced. In it we live and move and have our being. Let faith grasp that fact. Now, keep yourselves *in* that love, in the recognition of its reality, in the enjoyment of its comfort, in the sanctifying power of its purity. Keep yourselves *in,* not by your strength but by faith. Faith in God's love and power will keep you in Him, who is able to keep you from falling. But what are the means to be used? Those three sentences teach us this: "Building up," "Praying in," and "Looking for."

## NOVEMBER 23

*Whoso hearkeneth unto me shall dwell safely, and shall be quiet from fear of evil.*—Prov. 1:33

This describes the characteristics of the believer in his true condition. He has not only received the message which has been to him the "savour of life unto life," but he is continually receiving it. He is daily hearkening unto the LORD. This conditioning of hearkening must be maintained, if the blessings here described are to be a real and continuous enjoyment. What are those blessings? He shall *dwell safely.* He is kept by the power of God through faith unto salvation (1 Pet. 1:5). He is encircled by Him whose presence is salvation (Ps. 42:5, margin). He is guarded and shielded on every side by an armor that is impenetrable. He finds in God not only a refuge, but a Home, his Habitation, where he can *dwell.* But he is not only safe. He is free from corroding care, and from the "fear of evil." His mind is *quiet:* he is kept in perfect peace (Isa. 26:3). Oh, how much depends upon a listening ear and a yielded will! First, to know God's will, and then to be ready to do it. Hearkening implies all this. The spirit that hearkens is ready to obey.

## NOVEMBER 24

*My mother and my brethren are these which hear the Word of God, and do it.*—Luke 8:21

There is a family likeness between Christ and His people. His true relatives may be recognized by certain definite marks. They "hear the Word of God and do it." Godet observes on this passage: "The answer of Jesus signifies, not that family ties are in His eyes of no value (compare John 19:26), but that they are subordinate to a tie of a higher and more durable nature. In those women who accompanied Him, exercising over Him a mother's care (vv. 2 and 3), and in those disciples who so faithfully associated themselves with Him in His work, He had found a family which supplied the place of that which had deliberately forsaken Him. And this new, spiritual relationship, eternal even as the God in whom it was based, was it not superior in dignity to a relationship of blood, which the least accident might break? In this saying He expresses a tender and grateful affection for those faithful souls whose love every day supplied the place of the dearest domestic affection. He makes no mention of father; this place belongs in His eyes to God alone."

# NOVEMBER 25

*Being made free from sin, ye became the servants of right-*
*eousness.*—Rom. 6:18

Freedom from sin may be considered in three senses—freedom from its penalty, its power, and its presence. We are
free from sin in the first sense by justification; in the second
by sanctification; in the third by glorification. To ascertain
the sense in which it is referred to in any particular verse it is
necessary to look at it in connection with the context. In
this sixth chapter of the Romans the special aspect in which
sin is contemplated is that of a master; as one who seeks
to lord it over the soul, who would claim his service, and
would pay him wages ("the wages" which sin pays "is
death"). Freedom from sin in this chapter means freedom
from sin as a master. Identification with Christ in His death
delivers the believer from sin's authority. Sin henceforth
has no *right* to demand his service. Sin's claim has been
broken through our crucifixion with Christ on the cross.
We are now free to yield ourselves and our members to
God. That privilege must be intelligently apprehended by
the believer as his right, by virtue of Christ's death to sin,
and of the believer's identification with Christ in that death.

# NOVEMBER 26

*The* LORD *delighteth in thee.*—Isa. 62:4

It is one of the marvels of redeeming grace that God
should be willing to pardon the transgressor and receive
him into His presence; but it is still more wonderful that
He should look down upon him with complacency. "The
LORD taketh pleasure in them that fear him" (Ps. 147:11).
We must never forget, however, that this is true only as
we stand in Christ, or are in fellowship with Him. He
views us in His Son, and acquits us of every charge. He
sees us "justified from all things" in Him who is the LORD
our Righteousness. But in another sense, too, our heavenly
Father looks down upon us when we *abide* in Jesus Christ
for life and walk. He is well pleased with those who walk
in Christ, and are growing up into Him in all things. Then
it is that He delights in us. "The steps of a good man are
ordered by the LORD: and he delighteth in his way" (Ps.
37:23). That is, God looks with favor on the course that
such a man takes. It is our privilege to walk without blame
before Him in love. We shall hereafter be presented faultless, but even now we may be preserved blameless (compare Jude 24 with 1 Thess. 5:23).

# NOVEMBER 27

*The glory which thou gavest me I have given them.*—John 17:22

The Lord Jesus, in this wonderful prayer, refers to several gifts which the Father had bestowed upon Him. In the 2nd verse He speaks of a *people* given to Him; in the same verse, of *power* given to Him; in the 4th verse, of a *work* given to Him; and in the 8th verse, of a *message* given to Him. Then in the text we have the *glory* that had been given to Him. All these were the Father's gifts to His Son. Now this glory which the Father had given Him, the Lord Jesus declares He had bestowed upon His disciples. There was the glory of *Sonship*. That was the gift of the Father. "We beheld his glory, the glory as of the only begotten of the Father, full of grace and truth" (John 1:14). There was the glory of *union*. The glory of God tabernacled in the man Christ Jesus. And there was the glory of *fruit-bearing*. All these gifts of the Father to the Son, the Son now bestows upon His people. "God, who commanded the light to shine out of darkness, hath shined in our hearts, to give the light of the knowledge of the glory of God in the face of Jesus Christ" (2 Cor. 4:6).

# NOVEMBER 28

*As the body without the spirit is dead, so faith without works is dead also.*—James 2:26

As faith is a spiritual thing, and works are material, we might have expected that *faith* would have answered to the *spirit,* and *works* to the *body.* But the apostle, we observe, reverses this. He does not mean, of course, that *faith* answers to the body; but that "the *form* of faith without the working *reality,* answers to the body without the animating *spirit.* It does not follow that *living* faith derives its life from works, as the body derives its life from the animating spirit. Faith apart from the spirit of faith, which is *love* (and love evidences itself in *works*), is dead, according to St. Paul also" (1 Cor. 13:2).

"Plainly St. James means by *works* the same thing as St. Paul means by *faith;* only he speaks of faith in its manifested development; St. Paul speaks of it in its germ."

What Paul opposed in his argument was *self-righteousness;* what James opposed was *unrighteousness.*

"Not every one that saith . . . Lord, Lord, shall enter into the kingdom of heaven; but he that doeth the will of my Father which is in heaven" (Matt. 7:21).

## NOVEMBER 29

*We shall be satisfied with the goodness of thy house.*—Ps. 65:4

These words remind us of a passage in another Psalm (36:8), "They shall be abundantly satisfied with the fatness of thy house." Or, as Dr. Kay renders it, "They shall *overflow* with the fatness of Thy house." The thought is that there is such an abundant fullness of provision, that every want is met—every need supplied—and even this to an overflowing. It is one thing to be *safe*, it is another thing to be *satisfied*. Of course the first pressing necessity is that of safety. And so in the 36th Psalm, already quoted, we read, in the 7th verse, "The children of men shall put their trust under the shadow of Thy wings." There we see the soul under divine protection—safe. How blessed to be there, and to know that we are there! But we may also know what it is to overflow with the goodness of God's house—to be abundantly satisfied. Fullness of life and fullness of joy are the blessings which the Lord has secured for His people. It is when they are thus enriched that they are equipped for service.

"He satisfieth the longing soul, and filleth the hungry soul with goodness."

## NOVEMBER 30

*The Lord of peace himself give you peace always by all means. The Lord be with you all.*—2 Thess. 3:16

Notice the special title that is given us in this passage, "The Lord of peace." It occurs again in 1 Thessalonians 5:23, "The very God of peace himself sanctify you wholly"; and again in Hebrews 13:20, 21, "The God of peace that brought again from the dead . . . that great shepherd of the sheep . . . make you perfect in every good work." He has revealed Himself as the God of peace in the Gospel of His Son. The message He has sent us is the word of peace—"preaching peace by Jesus Christ." The work He has accomplished is the work of peace, "having made peace by the blood of his cross." The path into which He leads us is the "way of peace." In our text we have the apostolic prayer that the same Lord might Himself continually bestow upon these Thessalonian Christians the gift of peace. A perpetual gift of peace! Not at certain times of special devotion only—but "always." Not when circumstances are favorable only—"but by all means." That is, "in all ways." In dark and trying ways, as well as in bright and smooth ways.

# DECEMBER 1

*A man shall be as an hiding place from the wind, and a covert from the tempest.*—Isa. 32:2

"A man." Who is this man? It is "the second man—the Lord from heaven" (1 Cor. 15:47). This man is our hiding-place. "Jesus, Refuge of my soul, let me hide myself in Thee." There we are sheltered and safe from the storm of the law's condemnation, as well as from the assaults of Satan. "Thou art my hiding place; thou shalt preserve me from trouble; thou shalt compass me about with songs of deliverance" (Ps. 32:7). For every conceivable trial or trouble the Lord Jesus is the believer's refuge. "There shall be a tabernacle for a shadow in the daytime from the heat, and for a place of refuge, and for a covert from storm and from rain" (Isa. 4:6). It is the Lord's will that we should under all circumstances avail ourselves of this refuge. "He that dwelleth"—that is, he that "sitteth down," takes up his permanent abode, and does not merely use God as a *temporary refuge*—"He that [sitteth down] in the secret place of the most High shall abide under the shadow of the Almighty."

# DECEMBER 2

*Ye have an unction from the Holy One, and ye know all things.*—1 John 2:20

The Lord Jesus is referred to in this chapter under two important aspects—one in connection with His atoning sacrifice, and the other in connection with His anointing power. The first of these we have in the first verse of this chapter: "And if any man sin, we have an advocate with the Father, Jesus Christ the righteous." The righteous One; the One who fulfilled all righteousness; the One who met all the claims of a righteous law. He is the righteous One, as "He is the propitiation for our sins." Righteousness is the great idea that comes out in connection with atonement for sin and the fulfillment of the law.

But there is another aspect that is separate from the thought of sin altogether. Christ is the "holy One." As the righteous One, He fulfilled all the just claims of God's law as the Judge—as the holy One, He satisfied all the demands of God's heart as a Father.

It is from Him who hath received of the Father the plenitude of the Holy Ghost for His people, from Him who is the holy One, exalted to the right hand of the majesty on high—that the holy anointing flows to His people.

# DECEMBER 3

*I would seek unto God, and unto God would I commit my cause.*—Job. 5:8

Such was Eliphaz's counsel to Job in his affliction. It comes from a wise though perhaps not from a loving heart. As one has said, "Its only fault is that it implies an uncharitable and unjust reflection, as if Job was a prayerless man" (see 16:20; 10:2; 12:4; 13:20; 14:6). Job seems at times to have been so overwhelmed with darkness and confusion that he is hardly able to pray (23:3, 4, 15). And so many a child of God in the hour of greatest trial has been tempted to feel it is useless to tell out its trouble to God. Prayer seems so unreal, so powerless to bring down a blessing. And yet it is the soul's true resource. However cold the heart, however little it is able to realize the presence of God, or the nearness and sufficiency of His grace and power to save, to deliver, and to keep, this is the soul's best course, "I would seek unto God, and unto God would I commit my cause." If we *seek* we shall find; and when we find let us not only pray for His succor, but *commit* our cause to Him. How often we do much that falls short of this simple definite act. (See 1 Pet. 5:7; Ps. 37:5; Phil. 4:6.)

# DECEMBER 4

*Where shall wisdom be found?*—Job 28:12

In the eighth chapter of Proverbs wisdom is personified. It is not difficult to see that none other than the Messiah is intended, and that He is referred to there as the embodiment of divine Wisdom. As all holiness finds its center in God, so all wisdom is to be found in him in whom all the fullness of the Godhead dwells bodily. In Him are hid all the treasures of wisdom and of knowledge (Col. 2:3). Christ is made of God unto us wisdom (1 Cor. 1:30). "If any of you lack wisdom, let him ask of God" (Jas. 1:5). "Where shall wisdom be found?" We must seek it in the face of Jesus Christ. Nothing so helps us to grow in wisdom as being brought into purity and love. Let the affections be cleansed, let the thoughts and desires of our hearts be purified by divine love, and at once our spiritual perception is cleared, and our power to grasp the mysteries of revelation is strengthened. And so the apostle prayed, "that ye being rooted and grounded in *love,* may be able to *comprehend*" (Eph. 3:17, 18). Divine love is the soil in which the tree of knowledge grows.

## DECEMBER 5

*It is good for me that I have been afflicted; that I might learn thy statutes.*—Ps. 119:71

The Lord has two methods by which to lead His children on in the path of His will. By the guidance of His "eye," or by the discipline of the "bit" and the "bridle" (Ps. 32: 9). He does not afflict us willingly. He has no pleasure in our sufferings; but He loves us too deeply to withhold His chastisements from us, when He sees that through the perversity of our rebellious wills we prefer to follow our own path, rather than obey His guidance.

Present suffering is often the warning of more serious consequences ahead. Often the soul refuses to pay heed to these forebodings of coming ill, until far heavier and more terrible chastisements are brought down upon him through the depravity of his heart and the dullness of his conscience. It is not until the conscience is thoroughly aroused, and the sin, which has made the suffering necessary, is fully seen and confessed, that the soul is ready to learn God's statutes. "Before I was afflicted," such a one may truly say, "I went astray," and continued to go astray.

## DECEMBER 6

*It is God which worketh in you.*—Phil. 2:13

This is one of the facts of revelation which we are apt to pass over too quickly. We do not give ourselves time to take in all that is involved in this wonderful statement. If we are to take the words as meaning just what they say, then how marvelous is the fact here declared. It is GOD who is working in you. It is not a mere religious influence, but a Person—the Lord Himself. He is *in you.* He has come into the center of your being and taken possession of you, both to will and to work. This does not mean that you cease to exist, or that your personality is at an end. No, you are just the same responsible person you always were. But you give way to Him who is the true Owner of your whole being. He now takes the place you yourself once occupied. *You* were once in the center, but now Christ is your Center, and you can say, "He liveth in *me.*" The "I" or the "me" still exists, but the living Lord is in the center of the "me." Let that be true of us, and we can see how the power needed for the working is sufficient and continuous, because it is not ours, but His.

## DECEMBER 7

*He hath made him to be sin for us, who knew no sin; that we might be made the righteousness of God in him.*—2 Cor. 5:21

Chrysostom remarks on this passage: "The word 'righteousness' expresses the unspeakable bounty of the gift; that God hath not given us only the operation or effect of His righteousness, but *His very* righteousness, His very self unto us. Paul does not say that God treated Christ as a *sinner,* but as *sin,* the *quality* itself: in order that we might become not merely *righteous men,* but the *righteousness* of God in Him." This is the essence of the Gospel. It reveals to us the grand secret of the way in which God could be just and yet pardon the sinner who puts his trust in Jesus Christ.

The sin that shut us out of the presence of the holy God is not passed over uncondemned. It was laid upon Jesus Christ. He was made sin. He who knew no sin, who was a complete stranger to sin, became in the eye of divine Justice the very embodiment of sin itself, and as such received the penalty it deserved. It is on Him that sin was dealt with, once for all; and this that we might become the righteousness of God in Him.

## DECEMBER 8

*By love serve one another.*—Gal. 5:13

All true service springs out of liberty; that is to say, there must be freedom before there can be real acceptable service. "Ye have been called unto liberty; only use not liberty for an occasion to the flesh, but by love serve one another." This cuts at the root of all selfishness. It is the principle of divine love. "Seeketh not her own" (1 Cor. 13:5). It is one of the chief characteristics of the mind of Christ. "Look not every man on his own things, but every man also on the things of others" (Phil. 2:4). "By *love,"* not by knowledge only, *"serve* one another." This service shows itself in various ways. Perhaps sympathy and help are needed, then "Bear ye one another's burdens." Where wrong has been done, or feelings have been wounded, then "Confess your faults one to another," and "Pray ye for one another," "Forgiving one another." Where conflicting claims are clashing, then "Forbearing one another," "In honour preferring one another." "In lowliness of mind, let each esteem other better than themselves."

# DECEMBER 9

*To do justice and judgment is more acceptable to the* LORD
*than sacrifice.*—Prov. 21:3

Was not *sacrifice* appointed by Jehovah Himself? Were not
all those Levitical ordinances divinely instituted? And was
not their observance divinely commanded? Undoubtedly.
But they were not intended to take the place of that moral
obedience which the law of God had from the beginning
required. These outward "shadows of good things to come"
were often sadly abused. There were those who substituted
the external form for the inward spiritual condition. Nay
more, there were those who multiplied outward ceremoni-
als as a set off to sinful indulgences. "The 'Corban' sacrifice stood in the room of filial obligation. The lesser services of 'anise and cummin' were scrupulously observed to
the neglect of 'the weightier matters of the law—*judgment,
mercy, and faith'* (Matt. 23:23). Justly therefore did our
Lord commend the 'discretion' of the Scribe, who gave the
due place and proportion to the ceremonial and moral
service (Mark 12:34). Both are His requirements; and a
soundly instructed conscience will aim at both."

# DECEMBER 10

*No man is able to pluck them out of my Father's hand.*
—John 10:29

The safety of God's children does not rest on their own
attainments, or even on their own fidelity and decision, but
on the power of God. However great may be the strength
of our enemies, or however subtle their efforts to overcome the believer, it is our comfort to know that none can
pluck them out of our Father's hand. It implies that we
are being held up by God Himself. "Hold Thou me up,
and I shall be safe." "I will uphold thee with the right
hand of my righteousness" (Isa. 41:10). Here is the secret
of our comfort—not what we are or hope to become, but
what God is. "I know whom I have believed, and am persuaded that he is able to keep that which I have committed unto him against that day" (2 Tim. 1:12). The ability
of our God is the ground of our confidence. Greater is He
that is with us, than all those who can be against us.

"I am persuaded," said the apostle, "that neither death,
nor life . . . nor any other creature, shall be able to separate
us from the love of God . . . in Christ Jesus our Lord."

# DECEMBER 11

*Let not then your good be evil spoken of.*—Rom. 14:16

These words should be taken with the context. The apostle is referring to the liberty they had as Christians as to Jewish meats and days. That liberty was well founded, and so might be called "good." But it might be evil spoken of by reason of the evil it does to others. This they were to do all in their power to prevent. They were not to be indifferent as to whether their conduct would be misunderstood. They were to take pains to give no offense. "Abstain," says the same apostle, "from all appearance of evil" (1 Thess. 5:22). Again, the Apostle Peter says, "For so is the will of God, that with well-doing ye may put to silence the ignorance of foolish men" (1 Pet. 2:15). "Take heed lest by any means this liberty of yours become a stumblingblock to them that are weak" (1 Cor. 8:9). The matters referred to were questions of conscience. To act against one's conscience is sin. There was this danger lest through their liberty touching meats they should tempt weak brethren to act against their conscience. It is here that watchfulness and consideration for others are so necessary.

# DECEMBER 12

*The* LORD *thy God in the midst of thee is mighty.*—Zeph. 3:17

Two facts are stated here, What He is, and where He is. He is the Lord thy God. He is mighty. This implies covenant relationship. He is *thy* God. And this mighty One takes up His abode in the midst of His people—and in the heart of each believer. All things are therefore possible to him who is thus possessed. The Lord Himself dwells in them to save and to keep.

Can we say that we have thus enthroned Him in our hearts? The Holy Spirit strengthens us to this end, that Christ may dwell in our hearts by faith (Eph. 3:17)—that He might take up His permanent abode in our hearts. Thus enshrined He controls the whole being, and transforms the outer life, as well as the inner experience. "He will save." That refers to a daily and continuous salvation—a perpetual deliverance from sin's power and service. It is in this salvation that we find the fullest joy, because we are being preserved blameless, and kept continually in the light of God's countenance.

## DECEMBER 13

*Be strong in the grace that is in Christ Jesus.*—2 Tim. 2:1

Where is the strength with which we are to be empowered? It is in Christ Jesus. It is in no sense in ourselves. Power is not given to us as something to be used independently of Him. It is *divine* power, both as to its exercise and its source. Then, again, we are not called upon here to strengthen ourselves, but rather to allow ourselves to be strengthened. It is in the passive voice. "Be strengthened in the grace that is in Christ Jesus." It is the office of the Holy Spirit of God thus to strengthen us. He does this by bringing us into the center and source of all power. It pleased the Father that all fullness of grace should dwell in Jesus Christ. It is to Him the Spirit leads us. It is of the things of Christ that the Spirit takes and reveals to us (John 16:14). It is His might that He communicates to us. But as we said, not apart from Him, but in union and communion with Him. "Being strengthened with all might according to the power of his glory" (Col. 1:11). When we are thus strengthened, we have no consciousness of strength in ourselves. It is then that we know our own weakness. But we have the power of Christ.

## DECEMBER 14

*Make his praise glorious.*—Ps. 66:2

Or, as Dr. Kay renders it, "Ascribe glory in your praise of Him" (compare Isa. 42:12). "In praising Him, recognize *His glory*. To dwell on His kindness to us personally is good and right; yet it is not the highest style of praise. That requires us to set His holy and glorious Being before us in all its grandeur and elevation" (from *Von Gerlach*). Mark the difference between prayer and adoration. When we pray, our thoughts are more or less centered on our own need and on the supply of that need. But when we worship Him, our thoughts are fixed on the Lord Himself. His glory and majesty, His power and goodness, fill the whole horizon of our spiritual vision. Then it is that we praise Him, not merely for what He does—for His gifts to us—but for what He is—for the infinite perfections of His character. In praising Him, let us thus recognize His glory. We have been created and redeemed that we should be "to the praise of the glory of his grace" (Eph. 1:6). "This people have I formed for myself; they shall shew forth my praise" (Isa. 43:21). "I will praise thee, O Lord . . . I will glory thy name for evermore" (Ps. 86:12).

## DECEMBER 15

*Bear ye one another's burdens, and so fulfil the law of Christ.*
    —Gal. 6:2

"If you must needs impose *burdens* on yourselves, let them be the burdens of mutual sympathy. If you must needs observe a *law,* let it be the law of Christ" *(Bishop Lightfoot).* "These are the burdens I would have you bear— not the vexatious ritual of the law, but your neighbor's errors and weaknesses, his sorrows and sufferings" *(Ibid).* Cultivate a tender sense of brotherhood. We who are joined to the Lord are members one of another. We cannot have the mind of Christ and be indifferent to the sufferings and difficulties of others. "Look not every man on his own things, but every man also on the things of others. Let this mind be in you, which was also in Christ Jesus" (Phil. 2:4, 5). The Lord Jesus came to be God's faithful servant. He "came not to be ministered unto, but to minister, and to give his life a ransom for many" (Mark 10:45). This is to be manifested in our prayers, and in our efforts. In intercessory prayer, we should seek to identify ourselves with others in their difficulty.

## DECEMBER 16

*Having loved his own which were in the world, he loved them unto the end.* —John 13:1

Here is a distinction between Christ's people and the world. His people are the objects of His special love; He regards them as "his own." They are His peculiar treasure. For a time they are left to be in the world, and yet they are not of it. They are placed there to serve Him and represent Him. His love to them is unchanging. He loves them to the end—to the uttermost. What He did for His disciples at this time was deeply significant. It represented what He would do for His people hereafter. He washed their feet. So great is His love to us, that it is this that He is still doing for His disciples now. Our most humble walk, or holiest obedience, needs His continual washing. We are *His.* He has bought us with His own blood. He has loved us with an everlasting love. His grace has triumphed over us, so that we are His, not by purchase only, but by power—by renewing and transforming power. And the love that constrained Him when He died to redeem us is the same love that goes forth unceasingly to renew and to cleanse, to transform and to keep, until we shall appear with Him in glory.

## DECEMBER 17

*Quicken us, and we will call upon thy name.*—Ps. 80:18

Dr. Kay renders it—"Thou shalt revive us, and we shall call on Thy name." It is the mark of a revived and awakened soul that it begins at once to call upon God with reality and power. All coldness of spirit and formality are at an end. The beginning of such a revival is seen in the soul's desire to be quickened. There is a sense of deadness, and a consciousness of weakness. The soul begins to cry to God for renewed vitality and power. And when the fullness of life does come, nothing is more marked than the change that takes place in the soul's intercourse with God. There is a joy of heart and a freedom of spirit before the throne that were never known before. "Wilt thou not revive us again: that thy people may rejoice in thee?" (Ps. 85:6). Looking at the preceding verses, we notice how this thought runs through the whole Psalm (80). "Turn us again, O God, and cause thy face to shine; and we shall be saved" (v. 3). The same words occur again in verse 7, and with a slight modification in verse 19, and in verse 14.

## DECEMBER 18

*Let us therefore come boldly unto the throne of grace, that we may obtain mercy, and find grace to help in time of need.*—Heb. 4:16

To whom is this exhortation addressed? What is their spiritual standpoint? They are addressed to those who had come to the place of atonement. The brazen altar was the type of the cross—the place where the life of the victim was sacrificed, where the blood was shed, where the atonement was made. To that point these Hebrew Christians had come. It was the standpoint of the Jew who saw nothing but the shadow. It was the standpoint of the Hebrew Christian who, having grasped Christ as the substance, was in danger of coming short (Heb. 4:1) of the further privileges that belonged to him under the Gospel. It is to such the exhortation comes—"Let us come boldly unto the throne of grace." You have come to the brazen altar—now draw near to the mercy seat. The way into the holiest is now made plain. The veil is rent in two. Our High Priest has entered in before us. The blood is sprinkled all along the way right up to the throne—yea, on the mercy seat itself. That is the place of *worship*—the other is the place of atonement.

# DECEMBER 19

*Unto the upright there ariseth light in the darkness.*—Ps. 112:4

Light and darkness are often employed in Scripture as symbols of opposing moral conditions. Light is the emblem of holiness, of certainty, of joy. Darkness, on the other hand, is the symbol of sin, uncertainty, and sorrow. The text declares that on the upright God's light will shine. By the upright we must understand not a sinless condition of soul, but a state of *thoroughness*. The morally upright are those whose posture is erect, honest, and sincere toward God. This is what God required of Abraham, "Walk thou before me, and be thou perfect"—i.e., upright, thorough. They are upright in heart (Ps. 97:11). There may be seasons of darkness, in the sense of no assurance, no sensible comfort, no outward signs of God's presence; but there need be no darkness in the sense of actual estrangement through conscious transgression. This darkness is described in the words, "Who is among you that feareth the LORD, that obeyeth the voice of his servant, that walketh in darkness, and hath no light? let him trust in the name of the LORD, and stay upon his God" (Isa. 50:10).

# DECEMBER 20

*He hath chosen us in him before the foundation of the world.*
    —Eph. 1:4

"As with the Old so with the New Israel the choice is emphatically sovereign; not according to our works" (2 Tim. 1:9). On the other hand, it *takes effect* through means; a truth perfectly harmonious with sovereign purpose, while often conveyed in the language of ordinary contingency. Compare 2 Tim. 2:10; and, by way of illustration, Acts 27:22, with 31 (*Bishop Moule* on the Epistle to the Ephesians). The truth here expressed is emphatically the truth for those who have already been brought to a knowledge of the Lord Jesus Christ as their Savior. Every child of God realizes as he looks back, that it is all of God's sovereign grace that he is a believer at all. "The Divine prescience and predestination are not incompatible with human responsibility. Man is free, perfectly free, for his moral nature is never strained or violated. Foreknowledge, which is only another phase of electing love, no more changes the nature of a future incident, than after-knowledge can affect an historical fact."

## DECEMBER 21

*The days of thy mourning shall be ended.*—Isa. 60:20

Prophetic words concerning Israel. But they have a voice for God's children today. The passage describes the transition from a state of "violence" and "wasting"—of darkness and gloom—into a condition of light, and joy, and boundless prosperity. The soul may read in the history of God's dealings with His ancient people the counterpart of his own experience. The great principles on which He dealt with them in relation to their backsliding and sin are precisely those on which He deals with His spiritual Israel today. So the apostle declares, "Now all these things happened unto them for ensamples: and they are written for our admonition, upon whom the ends of the world are come" (1 Cor. 10:11). There is a time coming when the day of our mourning shall cease, and God shall wipe away all tears from all faces. But we need not wait until glory for *a* fulfillment of these words in our own experience. We may have a foretaste, in a measure at least, of the joy and blessing contained in these words. Fullness of joy belongs to His children even now (John 15:11).

## DECEMBER 22

*Your work of faith.*—1 Thess. 1:3

All real work springs out of faith as its root. For true acceptable service is work wrought in God, that is, in the strength of God. To have that strength so that it works in us both to will and to do, there must be the contact of faith. Faith brings us in touch with Him, who is the Fountain of all spiritual energy. Virtue, or power, goes out of Christ when the helpless soul is brought by faith in contact with Him. And that power at once begins to work. The work that follows, and is manifested in the service rendered by the believer, is the "work of faith." Faith and works are often contrasted, as if one meant inaction, and the other real effort. And yet how often is there intense effort without acceptable service. No service is acceptable to God which is not the "work of faith." Faith makes the soul receptive. And to become receptive we must learn to be restful. To receive the power and fullness we need, we have but to present an open channel, a free passage, a longing heart. All our supplies are in Him. If we are straitened, it is in ourselves, for we cannot be straitened in Him.

## DECEMBER 23

*Let him take hold of my strength, that he may make peace with me.*—Isa. 27:5

If any wish to cease from that ruinous opposition to divine love, here is an opening granted them for doing so.... "Let a man lay hold of My strong refuge":—let him flee to My altar of reconciliation (compare 1 Kings 1:50). He may escape My "severity," if he will embrace My "goodness" (Rom. 11:22) (*Dr. Kay* in the Speaker's Bible). When we lay hold of Christ, who is the power of God, we find peace with God. But the words in our text do not mean that the sinner has to make peace with God—for the true rendering is, "Let him make peace for me." God is here inviting the sinner to make peace *for Him;* "as if He were the party who sued for cessation of hostilities" (compare 2 Cor. 5:20).... "Let him assure Me by a solemn league (Josh. 9:15, same word) that he will not again wage war with Me; for he is the aggressor. I have provided a covenant of peace (Num. 25:12), to be administered by the Prince of Peace (Isa. 9:6), who in His own person will bear 'the chastisement of their peace' (53:5). I have issued a proclamation, 'Peace! Peace!' " (26:3).

## DECEMBER 24

*If ye live after the flesh, ye shall die: but if ye through the Spirit do mortify the deeds of the body, ye shall live.*
—Rom. 8:13

"Ye shall live." That "applies to every moment of the believer's existence on to the state of perfection" *(Godet).* Life here on earth in its highest and truest sense. But how is this life secured? By mortifying the deeds of the body.

"Mortification of sinful habits is not accomplished either solely or primarily by bodily exercise, human efforts, and fasting, but by Divine grace. Yet we must be workers together with the Holy Spirit in bringing the body into subjection."... "It is the plucking out of the right eye, and cutting off the right hand (Mark 9:43-48); the purging out the old leaven (1 Cor. 5:7); the rough dress of Elijah and John the Baptist (2 Kings 1:8; Matt. 3:4); the vow of the Nazarite (Num. 6:1-9); and the expulsion and extirpation of the Canaanites from their land" (Num. 33:55; Judg. 2:2, 3). The verb "put to death" is in the present tense, and indicates a continued process of resistance and self-denial *(Bishop Moule).*

# DECEMBER 25

*The kindness and love of God our Saviour toward man appeared.*—Titus 3:4

It is to the "kindness and love of God," and not to any merits of our own, that we owe our salvation. "We neither did works of righteousness, nor were saved in consequence of them: but His goodness did the whole" *(Theophylact)*. Every blessing is traced up to our Savior God. The Gospel is a revelation of the kindness and love of God. It is a manifestation of His grace in the glory of His righteousness. Justice and truth are seen in perfect harmony with mercy and peace. The salvation of the sinner is accomplished by the same act that magnifies every attribute of the divine character. The believer is privileged to behold, as he advances in a knowledge of salvation, how his own spiritual well-being and the glory of God are interwoven.

"The distinction between 'goodness' and 'friendliness towards men' is, that the former expresses the Divine *benevolence* in general, the latter more specially His *compassion* for mankind; so that both, taken together, are identical with *grace*" *(Lange)*.

"For the grace of God that bringeth salvation hath appeared to all men" (Titus 2:11).

# DECEMBER 26

*Be ye stedfast, unmoveable, always abounding in the work of the Lord.*—1 Cor. 15:58

See that ye turn not aside through the waywardness of your own hearts. Let there be a fixity of purpose, a decision of character, which shall keep you in the same course and with the same definite aim. Many there are who lack this characteristic. They are earnest and zealous for a while, and then seek another object of pursuit. They love change, and never continue long in the same course. Be ye "unmoveable"; that is, when pressure comes upon you from without. You may have no desire to turn aside. You may seek to keep before you the one and the same glorious purpose, "for to me to live is Christ." And yet, because of the influence of others, you are continually being hindered, and are often turned aside. "None of these things move me," said the apostle, when threatened by the prospect of suffering, and warned against pursuing his course. It is this decision of heart, and courage of faith, that are so essential, if we would always abound in the work of the Lord.

# DECEMBER 27

*We look not at the things which are seen ... for the things which are seen are temporal; but the things which are not seen are eternal.*—2 Cor. 4:18

We see from the context that the main thought of the passage is the spiritual transformation of our character. The outward man perishing—the inward man daily being renewed. This should go on continually. But it is conditional. It is *"while* we are looking not at the things which are seen, but at the things which are not seen"; in other words, it is while we are living and walking by faith— while we continue to see Him who is invisible. The believer lives in two worlds at once.

There is the outward world of sense. Of course he is not unconscious of the things that are seen. And there is the invisible world of faith. The unseen is as real as the seen—nay, because the things which are seen are temporal, and the things which are not seen are eternal—it is the unseen world that is the true and the real—the visible is but the shadow. As we live surrounded by the things that are seen, let us not look *at* them, but *through* them.

# DECEMBER 28

*Thy sins be forgiven thee.*—Mark 2:5

Our Lord spoke to the man's deepest need. He began with the disease of his soul. What the man was physically was only a picture of what he was morally and spiritually. Christ had all power over both spheres. Men were looking at the man's temporal misery. Christ was occupied first of all with the man's eternal welfare. They would have been content had our Lord granted only the bodily cure. But our Lord had a higher aim and a grander purpose in all His miracles of healing than the mere restoration to physical health. His miracles were signs, that is to say, they were significant of something higher than the temporal benefits they conferred. And on this occasion He would teach them that He had power on earth to forgive sins; a prerogative which the Jews justly believed belonged to God alone. That He could forgive sins, the miracle of healing was a proof. And the fact that He could forgive sins, was a witness to His deity. "I, even I, am he that blotteth out thy transgressions for mine own sake, and will not remember thy sins" (Isa. 43:25). "Blessed is [the man] whose transgression is forgiven" (Ps. 32:1).

## DECEMBER 29

*Understanding what the will of the Lord is.*—Eph. 5:17

God's will is described in Romans 12:2 as "good, and acceptable, and perfect." Practical holiness consists in proving that will, that is, testing it. This does not point to a mere external or mechanical compliance with it. It includes an inward approval of it. It assumes such a change within the man, that by a holy instinct he not only discerns it, as it is revealed, but he welcomes it; and amidst conflicting influences chooses it as that which he prefers. Our text from the Epistle to the Ephesians brings before us the contrast between the dull and blinded sense of a low spirituality—"the unwise"—and the quick and enlightened perception of the consecrated soul. It is the one who "presents" or "yields" himself wholly to God, who consecrates his *body* with all its faculties and powers, as well as his spirit and soul, who alone can know what this discernment means in all the intricacies of life.

How often the believer is heard to say, "My difficulty is how to know what God's will is!" The Bible teaches that if we *will* to do God's will we shall *know* (Col. 1:9).

## DECEMBER 30

*Blameless in the day of our Lord Jesus Christ.*—1 Cor. 2:8

"The day of Christ" is a sort of technical phrase in the New Testament. It corresponds to the "day of the Lord" in the Old Testament. "Waiting for the coming of our Lord Jesus Christ." Christ's coming in glory brings into exercise faith, and hope, and love. It is our privilege to be kept blameless right up to that day. After that He will present us *faultless* to His Father (Jude 24). Preserved blameless now, and presented faultless hereafter. It is one of the marks that should characterize God's children, in their life of testimony on earth, through all the sin and darkness by which they are here surrounded, that they "be *blameless* and harmless, the sons of God, without rebuke" (Phil. 2:15). That the believer will often be blamed by those who belong to the world is true, but he need not be blameworthy in the sight of God. They will accuse, but let us so walk that it may be that they *"falsely* accuse our good conversation." There is grace sufficient in the Lord Jesus Christ, "that ye may be sincere and without offence till the day of Christ" (Phil. 1:10). And the secret of this is in verse 11.

# DECEMBER 31

*The* LORD *thy God bare thee, as a man doth bear his son, in all the way that ye went, until ye came into this place.*
—Deut. 1:31

Who were they of whom this blessed fact is declared? They were a chosen people, a redeemed people, a delivered people. The Lord who had brought them out of the house of bondage did not set them free that they might be a self-guided and self-governed people. Bondage, misery, and perplexity would inevitably have followed, had they been left to their own resources. The Lord had redeemed and delivered them for Himself. They were to be a people for His posssssion. We see here how God's gracious upholding follows immediately His work of redemption. And is not this the history of His dealings with His people today? He bears us as a man bears his son, in all the way that we go. As we meekly follow His guidance and confide in His keeping power, we have the comfort of knowing that it is divine Wisdom who plans our future, and leads us into the unknown future. He thinks of us, and provides for us as a father pities and cares for his children. Let this blessed fact assure our hearts as we enter into another year.

# INDEX